The Thinking Child

What characteristics do children need to become motivated to learn? How do children's experiences and relationships affect their cognitive development? How do you provide learning experiences that meet the developmental needs of every child in your care?

The Thinking Child thoughtfully discusses the key principles of children's cognitive and intellectual development alongside descriptions of everyday practice. It clearly explains the cognitive strategies that children use to acquire new knowledge, the development of cognitive milestones such as symbolism, memories and the imagination, metacognition and creativity along with research into how the brain processes information.

Throughout the book, the author considers the key characteristics of effective learning and shows how play is one of the primary mechanisms that children use to access new knowledge and to consolidate their emerging ideas and concepts. These characteristics are then applied to integral aspects of early years practice to show how practitioners can:

- motivate children to acquire new knowledge about themselves and the world around them;
- help children to develop their own ideas creatively and use this knowledge as a base to learn new things;
- reflect on their own teaching methods to encourage children's engagement, motivation and creativity through effective observation and planning;
- engage with parents and carers to help support children's learning at home whilst maintaining the values of the family;
- celebrate the uniqueness of each child and provide learning experiences that are appropriate for individuals with particular learning needs, be they physical, emotional or cognitive, to ensure that every child has an equal opportunity to succeed.

Emphasising the importance of understanding the theory that underpins children's cognitive development, this accessible text shows practitioners how they can use this knowledge to provide learning opportunities that nourish children's thinking and creative skills.

Pamela May is an Early Years Consultant and a former Senior Lecturer in Childhood Studies at Canterbury Christ Church University, UK.

Foundations of Child Development
Series Editor: Pamela May

An understanding of child development is at the heart of good early years practice. The four books in this exciting new series each take a detailed look at a major strand of child development – cognitive, social, physical and emotional – and aim to provide practitioners with the knowledge and understanding they need to plan ways of working with children that are developmentally appropriate. Clearly linking theory to everyday practice they explain why practitioners teach in certain ways and show how they can provide learning experiences that will help children to become competent and enthusiastic learners. Whilst the series allows for an in-depth study of each of the four major areas of development individually, it also demonstrates that they are, in reality, intertwined and indivisible.

Titles in this series:

The Thinking Child

Laying the foundations of understanding and competence

Pamela May

Routledge
Taylor & Francis Group
LONDON AND NEW YORK

First published 2013
by Routledge
2 Park Square, Milton Park, Abingdon, Oxon OX14 4RN

Simultaneously published in the USA and Canada
by Routledge
711 Third Avenue, New York, NY 10017

Routledge is an imprint of the Taylor & Francis Group, an informa business

British Library Cataloguing in Publication Data
A catalogue record for this book is available from the British Library

Library of Congress Cataloging in Publication Data
A catalog record for this book has been requested

ISBN: 978-0-415-52190-1 (hbk)
ISBN: 978-0-415-52191-8 (pbk)
ISBN: 978-0-203-12172-6 (ebk)

Typeset in Bembo and Frutiger
by Fakenham Prepress Solutions, Fakenham, Norfolk NR21 8NN

Printed and bound in Great Britain by
TJ International Ltd, Padstow, Cornwall

Contents

Acknowledgements

I would like to dedicate this book to the Pilgrim Partnership, an early years school centred PGCE course, based in Bedford. The training, pastoral and administrative teams, together with their recently retired head of Initial Teacher Training, Martin Thompson, have consistently produced early years specialists of the highest quality. Teachers graduating from this programme, with their masters' strand in child development, are leading early years practice with a knowledge and commitment that inspires both the colleagues they work with and the children they teach. I am proud to have been associated with this programme since its inception.

My thanks, as ever, are due to John May for his editorial skills which have been invaluable in the production of this book and the others in the series. He has been enthusiastic throughout as well as patient and kind.

I have learned much from being with my grandchildren. The times we have shared have provided me with many examples of how children learn and develop so I am grateful to Millie, Jacob, Daisy, Albert and Arthur for sharing with me their unconditional love and their companionship. I am also grateful for letting me use their photographs and conversations.

Introduction to the series

Let us begin by considering two situations with which we are all probably familiar. Picture, if you will, a sandy beach. The sun is shining, there are gentle waves, little rock pools and a big cave. You have with you children aged six and three, a picnic, towels and buckets and spades. Having chosen your spot you settle down with a rug and a good book, occasionally advising about the construction of the moat for the sand castle or checking out the dragons in the cave. The children come back occasionally to eat or drink and there are the necessary breaks for toilets

Figure I.1 *Checking out the dragons in the cave*

and ice creams. By 4pm everyone has had a perfect day; you included. No one has cried, there were no squabbles and the children are happily tired enough to ensure a good night's sleep. For days and weeks to come they remember the '*best holiday ever*' as they reminisce about the castles they constructed and the dragons they frightened.

Now, transfer these same two children to a local supermarket. Imagine the scene here. In my experience the situation starts badly as I issue the firm instruction '*not to touch anything*' as we enter the store, and rapidly goes downhill as one child finds the strawberry yoghurts but the other wants the blueberry ones. I want the mixed pack because they are on offer and a three-way dispute is quickly under way. The smaller child is transferred to the child seat in the trolley, kicking and wailing loudly, and mothers look at me with either sympathy or distaste as this noisy gang proceeds with the shopping. Matters are not helped by the sweets displayed at the checkout at child level, which this cross granny does not consider either of them has deserved.

Why are these two scenarios so very different? The answer lies in the ways that children are hard-wired to learn about their world and to make sense of it. This process is called child development. Children are born with a set of strategies and they apply these strategies wherever they find themselves. One of the ways children learn is by using their senses, so they need to touch things that interest them to find out about them. That is fine when they are digging in the sand on the beach and collecting shells but not nearly as acceptable when investigating packets of crisps in a supermarket. Children are also hardwired to learn actively, that is, by exploring what is around them. Again, great when looking for dragons in caves but not such a helpful strategy around the aisles in a shop.

These books explore the strategies and other characteristics that all young children have and consider how they can be developed and strengthened in the course of young children's everyday learning.

This series of books is about the process of learning and not the content of learning. Each book describes a separate area of a young child's development and how their relationships and experiences affect the process of that development. Each of the four books takes one aspect and considers it in depth.

> **The Feeling Child**: *Laying the foundations of confidence and resilience.* In this book Maria Robinson considers children's emotional and behavioural development.
> **The Thinking Child**: *Laying the foundations of understanding and competence.* In this book I consider children's cognitive and intellectual development.
> **The Growing Child**: *Laying the foundations of active learning and physical health.* In this book Clair Stevens considers children's physical and motor development.
> **The Social Child**: *Laying the foundations of relationships and language.* In this book Toni Buchan considers children's social and language development.

Although each book takes one strand of children's development and looks at it separately, this is purely for the purpose of study. In real life, of course, children use all aspects of their development together as they learn to sustain friendships and communicate, grow taller and stronger, deepen their understanding of concepts and morals and grow in self-confidence.

There are thought to be certain characteristics inherent in all children that enable development to proceed effectively. Two of these inborn characteristics, for example, are motivation and autonomy. They need to be matched by an environment which supports their expression and development. Children who thrive and learn well will find their innate characteristics supported by loving and knowledgeable adults in a challenging yet secure environment. This environment will respect the fact that children learn through first-hand experiences, through their senses and that they will usually be doing this actively. This is why the beach provides such an effective learning environment and the supermarket less so. On the beach children can use their strategies of active engagement. They are motivated by the exciting surroundings and can play with considerable freedom and autonomy. Here one can see that their curiosity and capability of finding out about the world are perfectly matched by their environment.

This series will examine these ideas in depth. Established and current research threads through and underpins all the practical suggestions offered here. A theory is no use in isolation; it must always link to what happens to children wherever they are, every day. This is why these books will give the practitioner a chance to consider what implications their reading may have on their practice as well as giving them sound, evidence-based understanding as to why certain ways of teaching and learning can be so successful.

Central to this series are some key beliefs about young children. These include the premise that:

- children are potentially strong and autonomous learners
- they need loving and sensitive adults to be their companions
- children's view of themselves is key to their success as learners
- play is a powerful mechanism that enables children to develop their understandings
- what children can do should be the starting point of their future learning.

Perhaps these ideas are summed up most clearly in the last of the NAEYC principles:

> Children's experiences shape their motivation and approaches to learning, such as persistence, initiative and flexibility; in turn these dispositions and behaviours affect their learning and development.[1]

These principles are about not *what* children learn but *how* they learn and, consequently, how they are best taught. They are reflected in the new Early Years Foundation Stage (EYFS).[2]

The review of the EYFS by Dame Clare Tickell places much emphasis on the characteristics of effective learning that we considered above and it is these that we will be examining closely. Each book will discuss those characteristics which apply most closely to the strand of development being considered in the book but, of course, many of these will appear throughout the series. Each book will have chapters reflecting the EYFS emphasis on aspects of effective learning and, in particular:

- play and exploration
- active learning
- creativity and critical thinking.

Other chapters will cover aspects of practice common to all settings such as observing children's learning, engaging with families and how to provide for the different learning styles of girls and boys. Finally there will be a chapter that critically examines the notion of school readiness. Each author will explore what it means to be school ready and how we may best support Foundation stage children to take advantage of all that is on offer for them at key stage one.

Introduction to *The Thinking Child*

The Thinking Child sets out to examine some of the characteristics that children need in order to develop those skills particularly associated with cognition and the intellect. Early childhood is the time when new discoveries happen at the fastest rate. We know from neuroscientific research that children's brains are growing at great speed and any of us with young relatives will be familiar with the huge number of '*why*' questions that come our way. This physical growth of the brain prompts children to ask about their world and the rules that make it work. Their excitement about learning new knowledge is palpable and as practitioners we strive to provide environments that are challenging yet secure. The type of learning that will be explored in this book is described by Maria Evangelou as '*effective learning*'. That is, '*learning that engages the child at a deep enough level to hold the child's interest at the edge of their understanding thus motivating them to learn more*'.[1]

Some of the characteristics that help children to develop their thinking skills and their competence are, for example:

- positive dispositions
- reasoning
- predicting
- creativity
- engagement
- persistence
- flexibility
- understanding symbolism
- intrinsic motivation
- reflecting
- mastery orientation
- interdependence.

These attributes, and others like them, are life-long skills and have been proved to enable children to become successful adults who are likely to be self-reliant, resilient and independent. Children who do not possess these characteristics are at higher risk of finding challenge daunting, of possessing feelings of low self-confidence and of struggling with creativity and autonomy. If we, as early years practitioners, can introduce young children to these life-long skills and help them to use them every day, we will have given them tools and skills of inestimable value that they will use all their lives.

Setting the scene

The process of discovering how children come to understand the world in which they live requires us to look back in time. In this way we can see how ideas of childhood have evolved and how our current ideas have come about. This chapter will set the scene by exploring historical ideas of childhood and, in doing so, understand why current early years education and care looks the way it does.

There are many views of what childhood should be like, all of them invented by adults. No child comes into the world with an idea of what lies ahead. A child is born into a culture that will largely determine the sort of childhood that they will experience. An example of this is the islands in the Pacific where many three-year-old children are expert at using sharp knives to peel fruit; an idea that would horrify an adult from another culture. Even more controversial is the pride that some boys in Asian countries take in being included in the adult male practice of paid employment such as sewing footballs. It is often seen by them as a rite of passage into adult life rather than an imposition and a loss of childhood.

The wide range of evidence of child rearing through literature and paintings that are available to us might suggest that there are as many ways of raising a child as there are children to be raised. In our own culture, concepts of childhood have reflected this range, documenting both the joyous romanticism of the innocence that was childhood as portrayed in paintings such as Joshua Reynolds' '*The Age of Innocence*' in 1788. Contrast this with the extreme poverty and exploitation that accompanied the Industrial Revolution in the nineteenth century, graphically represented by the works of William Hogarth.

One of the earliest philosophers to publish work on how children should be raised and how best to educate them was John Locke in the eighteenth century. He was particularly interested in how children learned and he advocated the introduction of schools in which children could be taught during the part of the day when they were not working. His ideas may sound harsh to our ears, recommending that children from the age of three become accustomed to earning a wage, but he also recognised that '*learning might be made a play and recreation for children*'.[1] He thought that children were born with no innate characteristics and thus children's experiences largely shaped who they would become. This is sometimes known as the theory of the 'tabla rasa' or the 'empty slate'. Thus, it was thought to be vitally important to set a child on the right path early in life. This, in turn, had huge implications for child welfare and it was at about this time that the Foundling Hospital was opened in London by Thomas Coram. The Coram Foundation continues to work with children and their families in a range of ways to this day.

Locke's ideas were hugely influential and his theory that childhood was the foundation for a successful later life led to a common belief that children need to be filled with the knowledge, skills and culture that they would need as adults. The successful adult was seen as being literate, numerate and able to be trained so that a stable, well-prepared work-force would compete in the new, expanding economy. It was as the Industrial Revolution progressed, with its attendant need for adults who could read, write and add up, that the type of instruction known as 'skills and drills' emerged. There was no concept of education as a way of encouraging the population to become thinkers or to be creative. It was purely utilitarian and functional. We can read about these types of schools in the novels of the time. *Jane Eyre*, for example, gives a chilling account of life in Lowood school and describes how learning was delivered to large numbers of children in dreadful conditions.

The eighteenth century saw great changes in people's everyday lives as new ideas followed travelling explorers and contact through trade opened up other countries and other ideologies. The evangelical movement, which came in the wake of Martin Luther's break with the Catholic Church, brought with it a belief in original sin and the opening of Sunday schools which served to keep children safe when they were not at work or school. Sunday schools also instructed children in how to become '*neat, tidy, even obsequious, tractable, a favourite evangelical word*'[2] which was a far cry from the other major influence on children's upbringing which was holding sway at around the same time, that of Jean-Jacques Rousseau.

As so often is the case with beliefs and understandings, new ideas emerge to challenge the status quo. Rousseau, the French philosopher, had beliefs about children that were diametrically opposed to the improving and functional educational ideals of Locke and evangelicals such as John Wesley. Rousseau believed that children were self-regulating in terms of innate morality. They would search out beauty and goodness and were joyously innocent. '*Love childhood*', Rousseau suggested, '*indulge its sports, its pleasures, its delightful instincts*'. His view of an idealised childhood are to be seen in paintings of the time such as Sir Joshua Reynolds' *The Infant Samuel*, and *The Age of Innocence*, mentioned above. In these paintings children are seen clothed in white flowing robes, giving the appearance of angelic happiness. There is an atmosphere of calm and graceful simplicity, very far removed from the lives lived by the majority of working children of the time.

In Rousseau's famous book, *Emile*, he describes his idea of the perfect education. He suggests that children should not be taught facts and figures but that they should be free to discover all that the world has to offer for themselves. Children's individual personalities and characteristics should be allowed to develop and flourish naturally. There should be freedom from too formal instruction and children should be removed from big cities and placed in a country environment where they could roam freely. Rousseau's ideas have found a sympathetic response from many educators since he proposed them in the eighteenth century. The great educator, Friedrich Froebel, in particular, working in the first half of the nineteenth century, built upon Rousseau's philosophy, introducing the notion of the kindergarten or 'the garden of the children' where children's minds, souls, bodies, brains and spirits were nourished. Rousseau, and later, Froebel, recognised that children's development moves through certain stages and that it behoved educators to work with what was developmentally appropriate rather than trying to rush on to the next stage of learning. Froebel's phrase '*at every stage, be that stage*' suggested that the child should be encouraged to experience each level of learning to the full before being moved on.

The concept of developmentally appropriate stages was continued by Jean Piaget, a Swiss biologist working in the twentieth century. Piaget's ideas have, in recent years, been rightly challenged on many fronts but he retains his position as one of the greatest educational philosophers of recent times. Piaget was the first professional to study children scientifically. This gave him an opportunity to observe and study them with a lack of religious or political bias. Admittedly, his research was based only on his own children but his background as a developmental psychologist led him to the groundbreaking yet simple discovery that children do not think as adults do. He was the first researcher to suggest that each child individually constructs their own view of how the world works depending on their own experience of it. The stages of development that he identified formed the basis of teaching knowledge from the 1950s onwards. His idea of 'readiness' meant that a child would naturally pass on to the next stage of learning through their own discovery or through maturation. The teacher had little part to play in this process except to observe and record progress. In practice this meant that, as a teacher of a reception class in the 1960s, I did not give my non-readers books, as Piaget's theory would suggest that, as non-readers, it would make no sense to do so. Instead, they were given a small box containing flashcards which had to be learned by rote. Only then, when these words could be 'read', were the children deemed to be readers and to be able to benefit from a book. How educational theories change! Today we see babies coming home from their hospital births accompanied by a bag of books from the 'Bookstart' project which states that 'it is never too early to start reading to your baby'.

Aside from the negative implications of Piaget's theories, he gave us some significant understandings that underpin common good practice to this day. It is to Piaget that we owe the child-centred approach to teaching young children and the wisdom to match learning activities to children's present level of understanding. To him we also owe the notion of the child as an active discoverer of knowledge and this heralded the end, in the 1960s, of static whole-class teaching and rote learning for very young children which had held sway in the Board schools of the nineteenth century.

Piaget's work on how children construct knowledge has been deeply influential. He described how children gathered information through a process he called

When a new piece of knowledge came along, it would need to be [fitt]ed into what was already understood. If the new piece of knowledge [clashed] with existing knowledge a shift had to take place and the existing [knowledge] had to be adapted or confirmed. This process is also called accom[modation an]d it is the process whereby humans undergo a mental change in order [to solve p]roblems that, with our past level of understanding, were too hard to solve. Young children are endearing with what we call their misconstructs; their facts are not accurate but have been logically worked out in their minds based on existing understandings. Take, for example, the four-year-old girl who had been riding on granddad's tractor as he ploughed the fields in September, followed by a host of hungry gulls. When mummy asked what she had been doing she replied '*We were digging up seagulls*'; a very logical answer from her point of view and clearly constructed from the evidence of what she saw and her present level of understanding.

Perhaps the major dilemma that early years practitioners have had to consider is that the Piagetian method of gauging which level of development a child had reached implied that a certain level was 'normal' and that any different level was 'abnormal'. Thus, children began to be measured in terms of what they could not yet do rather than in terms of what they could do. The classic Piagetian example of this was his assertion that young children were egocentric and unable to see another's point of view. A later educationalist, Margaret Donaldson, repeated Piaget's experiments in natural settings rather than under laboratory conditions, and found that children were quite capable of taking on another point of view if they understood the question and what they were expected to do.

Some of Piaget's theories were also challenged by Lev Vygotsky, a Russian psychologist who published research during the twentieth century. One of the strengths of research into how children learn is that it covers a wide range of disciplines. Whilst Piaget considered children from the biologist's perspective, Vygotsky considered a more social aspect, suggesting that although children do make sense of the world individually, they do not, as Piaget believed, do it alone. We learn socially, thought Vygotsky, and he called children 'cultural apprentices' as they learn about their world from the adults around them. Later in the twentieth century, the academic disciplines of sociology and neuroscience have greatly contributed to our understanding of how children think and learn, giving us an ever more accurate picture of the early learning process. Continuing with the idea of children as social learners, Vygotsky believed that communication and language were central to successful learning. As practitioners, we recognise that those children who are the most confident learners are those who have a sufficient grasp of language to express their feelings and ideas.

Another aspect of social learning that Vygotsky highlighted was the role that the adult (sometimes called the '*expert other*') played in the learning process. Following the Piagetian model, the teacher observed and awaited 'readiness' but Vygotsky suggested another kind of readiness: '*Readiness in Vygotskian terms involves not only the state of the child's existing knowledge but also his capacity to learn with help*'.[3] Thus, the child's current level of understanding can be observed and at this point the expert can intervene and support the child to its next stage of understanding. This gap between what the child can do alone and what they can achieve with help, Vygotsky called the 'zone of proximal development'. It is at this point that much can be achieved by sensitive staff who can see what is the next step of learning for the child and can provide the support that is needed. This point has been recognised as being significant by the recent Effective Provision Pre-School Education (EPPE) research. Sustained shared thinking was described as '*An episode in which two or more individuals "work together" in an intellectual way to solve a problem, clarify a concept, evaluate activities, extend a narrative etc. Both parties must contribute to the thinking and it must develop and extend.*'[4] Sustained shared thinking supports the idea of a co-operative model of thinking which often has no pre-ordained outcome; in other words, the end result is sometimes surprising and not pre-planned. It is this type of thinking that can lead to creativity and metacognition (thinking about thinking).

Sustained shared thinking relies on an individual child's capacity or aptitude to learn from another person. Here is a prime example of where other aspects of a child's development interact with the intellectual area. Young children will only learn from their '*Important people*'[5]: their '*companions*' or trusted adults whom they know well. Thus, it is vital that each child has a key person at their setting with whom they can engage in this sustained shared thinking. A child who does not feel emotionally secure will be less inclined to explore new knowledge, which is often unpredictable. Emotional security plays a key role in the child's ability to go out on a limb and think in ways that may, or may not, be successful. Creative thinking is a risky business and failure must be acceptable; with the young child knowing that they will still be loved regardless of the outcome of the unpredictable business of exploring new knowledge and skills. Sometimes this area of thinking is known as '*If not, what if?*' and encourages a child to think of alternative solutions to problems. Stories are a good way to introduce this type of thinking in young children; I recommend *The Three Little Wolves and the Big Bad Pig* by Helen Oxenbury as a great illustration of the idea of alternative and creative thinking.[6]

Jerome Bruner, one of the giants of modern educational thought, is still working in the field of cognitive psychology .He believes, with Vygotsky, that learning is a social activity and he describes a rich early years setting as comparable to a scientist's laboratory where children explore, experiment and experience failure and success in a supported environment. The word 'apprentice' emerges again here as Bruner suggests that a child learns most effectively with an 'expert other', usually an adult, scaffolding or supporting the learning until the child has grasped the concept and no longer needs to be an apprentice. Bruner has debated different ways in which humans code information, calling them enactive (action-based), iconic (image-based) and symbolic (language-based). It is thought that all humans continually represent new knowledge in one of these ways, although with increasing maturity and competence the symbolic mode is increasingly used.

I remember, for instance, an occasion when I was called to an interview at a university campus. Not only did I drive to the campus the week before the interview date to be absolutely sure that I knew where the campus was (the enactive mode) and to find where I could park my car, but I also took a map (the iconic mode). Some weeks into my new post I dispensed with the map as I had successfully internalised the directions and had the confidence to arrive at my destination with no external aids. Admittedly, many people have a better sense of direction than I have and would not need these props but we can see, in children's play, the strategies they use to externally represent experiences that they have encountered in their lives. In the following chapter we will be exploring the part that play has in helping children to learn and, in particular, the ways in which pieces of thinking are knitted together by the use of external props, or schemas.

Bruner considered that, to some extent, children's learning could be hampered by the adherence to a belief in inflexible stages of development. He thought that any subject could be taught in some intellectually honest form to any child at any stage of development. For example, a young child who notices that flowers die without water can be helped to understand that plants take water up through their stems (perhaps by seeing coloured water changing the colour of a flower) but does not need to be told about the entire scientific process of osmosis. Using fruit to make alternating printed patterns can be thought to be the beginning of understanding about algebra, and caring for a pet gives valuable lessons in beginning to understand the differences between living and non-living things.

Leading on from the assumption that most knowledge can be translated into forms that young children can understand comes Bruner's theory that children's learning develops by having early and regular access to experiences at which they can repeat and gain mastery. This has significant implications for our practice as it means that we must let children find out how, for example, glue and Sellotape and scissors work *before* asking them to make a model. Only by revisiting these explorative processes can children gather the expertise to gradually build up the experience they need to feel confident enough to try something more complex. This is the way to what we call a '*mastery orientation*'. The delight that a child feels on completing something that is challenging builds into a 'can do' attitude to learning if it is felt on a regular basis. Bruner called this theory the 'Spiral curriculum' and it means that children will bring their increasing knowledge and expertise to whatever they are learning and grow ever more competent. An implication for us as practitioners is that we must provide resources on a consistent basis so that children have the opportunity to refine and practise their skills. Settings where things are changed around on the grounds that '*children will get bored*' are, in fact, hindering their early attempts to try the same thing again and again until it is perfected.

Both Bruner's and Vygotsky's theories of how children learn refute Piaget's notion that teachers need to wait until a child is around seven years of age before logical learning can take place. What children lack, we now understand, is not logic but experience. What we need to do to enable younger children to learn is to present knowledge in ways that make sense to them within the current levels of understanding that they have.

These ideas from those we call the great educators have given some clear messages to practitioners that will enable them to teach effectively. Indeed, theories are of little use, aside from general interest, if they do not influence practice. How, then, does a practitioner decide which theories are sound and reliable? Dahlberg, Moss and Pence discuss just this dilemma, suggesting that, as professionals, '*we embody theories, often without realising. In other words, we absorb theories to such a degree that they govern our ideas and actions, although we may not recognise what is going on – even to the extent of confusing theory with truth*'. They go on to comment that '*Theories, in short, are double-edged*'.[7]

A major problem with theories is that they can be used by politicians for short-term gains. At the end of the Second World War, the government used John Bowlby's theory on children's emotional attachment to their prime carer as part of their 'Hearth and Home' policy. This action brought working mothers back home from their wartime employment, thus preserving the few jobs available for returning soldiers. Currently, childcare could be seen as a factor in the labour market supply. One could question whether today's childcare drive is more about what is right for children than what is thought to be needed to ensure full employment. Childcare professionals often find themselves positioned uncomfortably between opposing theories. Angela Anning, in her book *The First Years at School* eloquently described the situation that was encountered in the 1990s. '*Infants teachers find themselves caught between the relentless currents of child-centred progressivism and utilitarian demands to teach the basic skills.*'[8] Some practitioners might conclude that, despite the Foundation stage of education now ending at age six instead of five, Anning's findings are still relevant. Wherever the divide exists between opposing theories, there is a tension as to how teaching and learning should happen.

A sensible way forward would seem to be to consider those theories that clearly link to children's development as the ones that can be most helpful in guiding teaching and caring for young children. The National Association for the Education of Young Children (NAEYC) has drawn up ten principles based on children's development and these have been enshrined in current legislation. The principles below are included in the introduction to this series and, together with the other five principles, form the basis of much current thought about early years education:

- children are potentially strong and autonomous learners
- they need loving and sensitive adults to be their companions
- children's view of themselves is key to their success as learners
- play is a powerful mechanism that enables children to develop their understandings
- what children can do should be the starting point of their future learning

These principles have come directly from what are known as 'social constructivist' theories and central to this belief is that learning is an active mental and individual effort to construct meaning. This belief does not sit well with what is often called the 'skills and drills' approach of the nineteenth-century Board schools which has seen such a resurgence since the 1980s. It does, however, have much resonance with two systems of early years education which are highly regarded in the twenty-first century, Te Whariki in New Zealand and the Reggio Approach in northern Italy. The pedagogies from both these countries regard the child as potentially '*strong and autonomous*' and believe that constructing understanding is a joint venture between learner and tutor. Although based in very different cultural environments, they place the child unequivocally at the centre of the education process. They consider the child's family and community as central to successful learning and they encourage children to make sense of their knowledge, experiences and ideas through imaginative and creative activity. These ideas link strongly with what we know about how children develop, and wise practitioners have always linked the ways they teach to children's natural development. What we also know from the newer discipline of neuroscience is that babies' and young children's brains light up when they are actively engaged with something that interests them. This would appear to vindicate what practitioners have long believed from their own observations of children's learning behaviour.

Finally, the current independent report on the Early Years Foundation Stage by Dame Clare Tickell places a high emphasis on what she calls '*characteristics of effective learning*', in other words, factors '*arising within the child which play a central role in learning and in becoming an effective learner*'.[9] These characteristics are in place in the current EYFS. They are:

- playing and exploring
- active learning
- creating and critical thinking.

They can be seen quite explicitly to reflect the theories of how children develop understanding and competency that we have considered in this chapter. By studying the historical context of early years education we can come to an understanding of how we have arrived at this point and can begin to make some decisions of our own about how we should help children to learn, based on truths and reliable research evidence rather than fashionable theories with short-term objectives. The ideas and theories that have been explored in this chapter will form the bedrock to the debates and discussions that will be found in the ensuing chapters.

CHAPTER 2

Playing, exploring and learning

This chapter is about engaging children in their learning. It discusses the central part that play has in enabling children to come to new understandings in safe yet challenging ways. It will consider their play as they use it to *find out and explore* new knowledge, and as they *use what they know to apply their knowledge* to new learning. It goes on to discuss how '*play helps children to develop strategies to try out new things*'[1] so that they can succeed, or fail, safely.

Play is a slippery idea! It defies simple definition and means different things to different people. For the purposes of this chapter it is necessary to unravel the tangle of meanings that are attached to play and to try to discover exactly what it is about the process of playing that is so powerful in helping children to learn new things. We know that play is highly regarded as a way to enable learning. The EYFS card 4.1 is uncompromising in the claim that '*In their play children learn at their highest level*' and Vygotsky talks of play as being '*the leading source of development*

Figure 2.1 *In their play children learn at their highest level*

in pre-school years.[2] Play, it would appear, has high status in both education theory and in the government documents that determine our practice. Yet we know only too well that play is often poorly understood by staff in settings and by parents and that confused thinking around the place of play as a tool for learning tends to lead to lack of challenge and stimulation. Researchers investigating the ways in which both children and adults spent their time during free-play sessions in nurseries in the 1980s found that '*there was a lack of challenging activity in children's free play, which tended to involve simple repetitive activities*'.[3] For us, as carers and teachers, it is not enough to repeat the mantra that the education of young children must be founded on play. We must understand what type of play enables learning and why this might be. This we will attempt to do by examining both the process of playing and the process of learning. By exploring these ideas we may come to some understanding of how it is that such high accolades are awarded to playful learning and how we can ensure that our practice is of a high enough quality to support these claims.

The nature of play

Play is a universal human function. If we are six or sixty, play offers the same opportunities to understand how the world works and to gain new knowledge. Consider the newly retired adult who has decided to grow her own vegetables. Gardening, like fishing, singing in a choir or learning a language are often hobbies for adults who have made enough time in their lives to study something they enjoy. What motivates a person to give considerable time and effort to improving their chosen skill? It is not usually money nor is it the pursuit of perfection but it is most likely to be the intrinsic pleasure that humans derive from having a go at something and building on progress. One of the reasons that hobbies are so satisfying is that they engage most aspects of our skill, understanding and abilities, leaving us feeling generally good about ourselves and looking forward eagerly to the next time we can go fishing, swimming or be out in the garden.

To engage fully with, for example, the business of creating a beautiful garden we will need to be engaged cognitively, physically and emotionally. We need to understand which plants will thrive in which part of the garden; this engages our intellect or our cognitive skills. We need to be physically fit enough to dig our garden and pull up the weeds. This engages us physically and will give us a feeling of healthy tiredness at the end of the day. We also need the motivation to persist with our hobby when things aren't going so well and to get outside when the sun is not shining and to think through problems when the birds eat our young seedlings! This ability engages the emotional aspect of our personalities so that we take part in quite a struggle and invest much effort, time and thought in our chosen hobby.

I hope that this sounds a familiar process because it is identical to the process that children are going through when they are playing. To take this analogy one step further, let us consider the three statements mentioned in the first paragraph of this chapter and apply them to my chosen hobby of gardening.

Finding out and exploring is one of the joys of gardening. I can walk outside my back door and look at what is there. I can dig up the soil and check how rich it is. I can look over my neighbour's hedge and see what grows well in his garden and I can check out where the sun shines so as to place my vegetable beds in just the right place for the best crop. I can find my local nursery and ask which seeds I should be planting and I can buy a gardening magazine for advice. Best of all, I can start planting seeds and cuttings and begin to find out what grows well and what doesn't.

Having had a garden before, I can *use what I already know and apply my knowledge* to my new garden. My existing knowledge about the sort of soil that I have found in my garden helps me to choose what plants to try out and my previous gardening experience tells me what tools I will need to buy. As there are no rules to my hobby I can do exactly as I please in my garden; I can make the decisions as to whether to try to grow some tender plants that might die if there is a severe frost.

However, because I am not new to gardening, I have *developed some strategies that I can use to try out some new ideas* so I will try wrapping my new olive tree in a straw blanket during the winter months in the hope that it will survive. If it does, I will be able to put this new knowledge to good use and grow other tender plants with more certainty. If it does not, and my olive tree dies, well, I have experienced a failure but I can learn from failure as well as success and that knowledge will help inform my plant purchases and care in the future. Throughout all these processes I have been deeply engaged in my hobby, keen to meet others with similar interests and happily receiving gardening tokens as Christmas presents.

We have examined this link between play and adult hobbies at some length but I hope that, by doing so, some of the aspects of this type of playful learning have become apparent. This type of learning is effective for many reasons, some of which are given in the Department for Children, Schools and Families' document *Learning, Playing and Interacting*.[4]

Glance down this list of the known attributes of play and check how many of them were apparent in the gardening analogy:

- finding an interest
- being willing to explore, experiment and try things out
- knowing how and where to seek help
- being inventive – creating problems, and finding solutions
- being flexible – testing and refining solutions
- being engaged and involved by concentrating, sustaining interest, persevering with a task, even when it is challenging
- making choices and decisions
- making plans and knowing how to carry them out
- playing and working collaboratively with peers and adults
- managing self, managing others
- developing 'can do' orientations to learning

- being resilient – finding alternative strategies if things don't always go as planned
- understanding the perspectives and emotions of other people.

In this book, we are concentrating on those aspects of learning that relate to intellectual or cognitive development but, of course, play lends itself to emotional or affective aspects of learning as well. The power of play lies in the fact that it is holistic. As well as learning new knowledge, it helps children (and adults) to work collaboratively and to develop empathy with others' views and emotions. These elements are fully explored in the companion books in the series.

Play, then, is one of the successful processes that humans of any age employ to understand how the world and its systems function. Recent brain research supports all that we, as early years practitioners, have long suspected about the nature of learning. That it is through personal experience that each of us constructs our own individual view of the world.

The nature of learning

Having considered some pointers about play and thought through some of the reasons that it has received such high accolades, it is time to connect play to the second part of the equation, that of learning and the ways in which humans learn most effectively.

Learning can be thought of as a journey. In New Zealand, for example, assessment of children's achievements is often referred to as 'a learning journey' as progress towards competence and secure understanding is charted. Learning can also be thought to be linked to *'bringing about change, or at least coping with change'*.[5] Change is, as we know from history, part of the human condition and our ability to cope with change is one of the main reasons that our species has survived.

Our increased understanding of the workings of the brain has enabled us to know with certainty that babies' experiences begin to settle into patterns that offer security and reassurance in the confusing early stages of life. Oft-repeated experiences form physical patterns in the brain. These patterns are caused by the brain cells, or neurones, talking to each other and making connections. The connection points are known as synapses and enable learning to develop in an infinite number of directions. The directions in which learning will develop are thought to depend both on inherited, or genetic, influences and experiential influences and what is learned will encompass all areas of development. The implication from neuroscience for practitioners is that the richer the experiences children have, the more connections will be made in their brains and the more opportunities the young child will have to develop a wide range of new knowledge. Each new understanding on a child's learning journey involves physical growth of the brain as well as a growth of self-confidence as the child enjoys the satisfaction of their increased cognitive powers.

A true story of Daisy, aged five

Daisy and her granny are on their way to a London park to feed the ducks. On the way they have to step around a flood of water which is gushing from a broken pipe and is flowing along the gutter. '*What's all that water, granny?*' asks Daisy. '*Well*', says granny, pointing to a nearby square hole in the road, '*I think it's the water from that house nearby but the pipe's broken so it's flowing down the drain.*' '*What's a drain?*' comes the reply. '*Well*', says granny, '*it's where the water runs underneath the streets to be recycled*'. At this point granny tries to move on towards the duck pond as she senses that this line of questioning might be getting somewhat challenging. Daisy, however, is rooted to the spot. '*How does the water get moved around underneath the streets, granny?*' '*In big pipes*' comes granny's reply. '*Where does the water go then, granny?*' '*Well*', says granny (clearly struggling in her efforts to be technologically accurate), '*it gets cleaned at a recycling plant and sent back to your taps*'. '*For us to drink?*' asks Daisy. '*Yes*' says granny, realising too late the horror that this explanation will cause. '*Yuk*', says Daisy, '*I'm only going to drink Ribena.*'

This example of a child learning some new knowledge is interesting on several levels. It illustrates the point that, as a piece of knowledge, it is not one that any practitioner would include in a programme of learning for a Foundation stage setting. London's water recycling system is not a subject that would immediately spring to mind as suitable for a five year old. Why, then, was it so interesting to Daisy? There are several reasons, one of which is that the questions about the water are all in Daisy's head and not in granny's head. Learning is at its most powerful if the learner is curious and motivated; this is, to all intents and purposes, what we might call child-initiated learning. At school, of course, the situation is usually reversed with teachers asking the questions and the children having to answer them. We know that, in child development terms, this is a much less powerful way of learning as one of the key features, that of motivation, is missing. Daisy is in the company of a loved and trusted adult who, she knows, will respond to her questioning with patience, if not always with complete accuracy! Another contributing factor is that Daisy is experiencing the gushing water at first hand; it is a real experience and one that captures her imagination because it is physically in front of her, there to be seen and felt. This was certainly an example of a rich experience and links with what Jerome Bruner meant when he suggested that '*any subject can be effectively taught in some intellectually honest form, to any child, at any stage of development*'.[6]

There are other links to theorists such as Vygotsky who placed both language and the teacher at the heart of learning. He viewed the most powerful learning as that which could be thought about using descriptive and questioning language and this is clearly the case in this illustration. The role of the adult is also seen as crucial, and certainly Daisy would not have learned what she did had a well-loved adult not been present to discuss the issues or if Daisy had been in the company of someone less well known to her. The mutual exploration of the subject with no particular objective in view is exactly what is meant by the term 'sustained shared thinking' and is a crucial factor in successful learning. EYFS card 4.3 is explicit in its description of this type of learning partnership. '*Sustained shared thinking involves the adult being aware of the children's interests and understanding and the adult and children working together to develop an idea or skill.*'[7] The implication for early years settings must be that the key person, a loved and trusted adult, is, as the name implies, key in transmitting new knowledge to a young learner.

This chapter places an emphasis on one of the earliest elements of learning, that of exploration. Certainly, Daisy's conversation about drinking water could be said to be in the category of *finding out and exploring*. This new knowledge was recalled quite soon afterwards as Daisy resolutely refused to drink tap water for a while (except, of course, in Ribena!). It may be that her knowledge remained stored in the frontal cortex of her brain, which deals with the learning of new concepts, perhaps to re-emerge in a game or as part of a story. It has joined the growing store of knowledge that she is adding to every day, ready to be recalled as and when it might be needed.

Theory about learning suggests that this new understanding might form the basis of another new concept. Perhaps Daisy will see some large pipes lying in a London street and remember her conversation with granny. She might wonder if these are water pipes, a conclusion that would not have been possible if the flood conversation had not happened. It is in this way that the synapses in our brains make new connections, as described on EYFS card 4.3, '*New connections help to transform our understanding*'. Applying her knowledge to the large pipes spotted at a later date would be an example of '*using what they know to apply their knowledge*' to new learning and it may well be that, at some point in the future, she will use a game in her play which involves some aspects of what she learned that morning on the way to feed the ducks.

It is worth considering that whilst Daisy was learning her piece of new knowledge, thus adding to her cognitive library, she was also learning about relationships. As young children are never without an adult, all their learning is mediated by adults and so relationships sit at the heart of all children's learning. Relationships are somewhat trickier to learn about than technological facts mainly because the patterns that are so reliable in science are much less reliable when applied to human behaviour. Young children need to test out their theories about who can be trusted so that they know who to turn to when they need help. It is for this reason that consistency in our behaviour when dealing with young children is so important. Those adults who are consistently responsive and who have time to engage with children will be those to whom children will turn most often when help is needed.

At the start of thinking about the nature of learning it was stated that fundamental to the notion of learning was the idea that it involved the ability to cope with change and this is an idea that warrants a little more examination. All learning involves a shift from the rather comfortable place we are in to the somewhat more challenging position of having to confront something we do not quite yet understand. For an adult this may be a new piece of knowledge, perhaps a new language or skill or a new concept, such as the nature of teaching and learning! Whatever is about to be learned, existing knowledge has to be adapted to accommodate the new understanding. Sometimes this is really hard. Suppose, for example, that as a practitioner, you believe that the decision making and control of young children should always lie with the adult. Discovering about child-initiated learning, autonomy and the equality implicit in sustained shared thinking on a training course might pose some challenges and cause some soul-searching. This process is sometimes called cognitive dissonance, where the learner has to wrestle with existing knowledge and make decisions about its value in the light of the new information being received.

Children have to cope with this all the time as they process new information and constantly assess it against that which they thought they knew. A considerable amount of emotional resilience is required as they have little experience with which to judge the new knowledge and often have to reject that which they felt certain about in favour of something that is only barely understood. Children will be constantly checking out whether what they thought they knew is accurate and we will all be familiar with the wide range and persistence of their questioning both in our professional and personal lives. This search for accuracy is part of the necessity to make sense of how the world works and is what all children spend the majority of their time doing. As stated earlier, oft-repeated experiences lay down patterns in the brain and this applies to relationships just as it does to the intellect. A practitioner who is inconsistent with young children will not be offering the security that the child needs to partner them in their learning journey.

Play for learning

Having considered both play and learning in some depth, it remains now to look at how they interweave to provide a valuable context for children's development. Play of a high quality, where children are engaged and thinking creatively, will provide the perfect medium for deep-level learning to take place. One of play's greatest assets is that the learning that happens whilst children are playing is holistic, just as it is in real life. In school, knowledge is often artificially broken down into subject areas so that children find themselves in one session learning about number bonds and a separate session cooking biscuits. In children's play they use their number bond skills for the real purpose of dividing the number of biscuits between the children present and in this way the learning has a purpose and makes sense to them. Loris Malaguzzi, in his poem 'The Hundred Languages of Children',[8] suggests that teachers tend to separate out and restrict the bodies of knowledge to which children have access. He makes an impassioned plea for children to be able to link differing aspects of knowledge together, for example *'reality and fantasy'*, *'science and the imagination'* and *'reason and dream'*. Play provides the exact conditions for these seemingly opposite aspects of knowledge to be fused together in the sort of unpredictable tangle that, in many cases, replicates life itself and the way we all live it, day by day.

The unpredictability of role play, in particular, allows children to experience one of the most difficult emotions of real life; and that is uncertainty. Playing helps children to practise being unsure and to develop resilience when things do not turn out as they had expected. Our lives are full of uncertainties on both grand and everyday levels and it is unhelpful to suggest to children that learning always consists of right and wrong answers. Just as adults build confidence and resilience to face the uncertainties that the future holds, children can be helped to develop confidence and resilience by playing out scenarios that have a range of possible resolutions. Intellectual development is just as much about developing the imagination as it is about remembering facts and figures. The scientist dreams of curing a disease by practical experimentation just as the artist creates fantastical images with tubes of paints and brushes. Without dreams there is little motivation to explore and experiment and without the imagination no statue, temple or book would ever have been created.

Play, then, gives children opportunities to give full rein to their imagination, a theme that will be explored more fully in Chapter 3. For the purposes of this chapter, where we are considering exploration which is sometimes thought of as the earliest stage of play, it may be helpful to remember that one of the joys of play, from the child's point of view, is that exploratory play rarely has an end product. Particularly in its early stages, the satisfaction that children get from playing is that they do not have to produce anything to show for their hours of concentrated playing. It is a wise practitioner who recognises that the child who is engaged deeply in their play is putting in a great amount of effort, concentration and persistence into their play and is developing increasingly refined skills. Sometimes these are cognitive skills, leading to the understanding of a new concept or idea and sometimes they are physical, emotional or social skills. They are all skills for life which need nurturing and it is during this time of finding out about the world that the child's disposition to develop these skills is laid down.

To support the young child in developing a positive disposition towards learning and to believe in themselves as learners, practitioners have a crucial role to play. By modelling an attitude which is sometimes called a 'confident uncertainty' they can suggest that not being certain is a normal state of affairs and that alternative ways of thinking are adding a rich dimension to their play. In this way children can experience failure without suffering despair; they will be able to have a go in the knowledge that they can learn from mistakes. In the pluralist world into which our children have been born, it is a combination of understanding practitioners and rich play experiences that will help them find their own strengths and interests and develop their belief in themselves as confident and competent learners.

Challenges and dilemmas

- How will you ensure that staff teams have a thorough understanding of play and its place in learning? Some lead practitioners ask colleagues to read an article or chapter to be discussed at a staff meeting. They might arrange visits to other settings.

- Providing playful experiences that encourage the full range of abilities and interests in your group is a challenge. Often broad themes such as 'Who lives here?' (see Chapter 9) enable children to join in at the appropriate point on their learning journey.

CHAPTER 3

Active learning

The locus of a young child's confidence is not in his thinking, although he enjoys being clever and knowledgeable. It is in his solar plexus, in his sense of himself as a physically active, feeling, coping, being.[1]

The characteristics of active learning have much in common with the ideas we encountered in Chapter 2 when thinking about adult hobbies. The term active in this chapter will be considered in its widest sense; that is, children being engaged actively both in their minds and through their bodies. In fact the characteristics of active learning, as described in EYFS card 4.2, place great emphasis on the mental attitudes that children need, such as the importance of *'feeling at ease, secure and confident'* and *'having some independence and control'*. These attitudes are some of those that will underpin children's ability to develop the confidence, motivation and curiosity to engage with their learning. Thus they will develop the tools of effective learning such as concentration, persistence and satisfaction that are all central to their progress. The aim of creating an early years environment in which children can feel secure, curious and engaged is to promote children's thinking skills so that they can think deeply and for a sustained period of time about a relatively small aspect of knowledge rather than encouraging a superficial coverage of a wide range of interests. We may have seen the child who is fascinated by how many legs there are on a spider. She will have spent a long time with a magnifying glass checking that the observed spider has the requisite number! This process shows a number of attributes that we should be pleased to see, all of them are active processes, both mentally and physically.

First we will think about what we want to achieve in our setting in terms of children's *thinking, understanding* and *competence*. These dimensions of learning are categorised in Dame Tickell's review of the Foundation Stage as having three parts. They are:

1 Being involved and concentrating
2 Keeping on trying
3 Enjoying and achieving what they set out to do.

Each of these three aspects is necessary for a child to be able to think, understand and develop confidence and, after attempting to clarify their meanings, we will consider the practical ways in which we can encourage these attributes to develop as we work with our children on a regular basis.

Thinking

The process of thinking is rather like having a conversation with yourself. A working knowledge of language is useful so that ideas and feelings can be tossed around and adopted or rejected as they are matched with existing understandings. To be able to concentrate requires several attributes such as attention, motivation and confidence. These are sometimes known as *cognitive skills* or *habits of mind* and they will stand children in good stead for their entire lives. The skill of attention requires children to notice what is interesting in their world and this will usually need adult input. The girl counting the spider's legs above is likely to have had, at some point, an adult bring her attention to a spider and to have had a conversation with her about how many legs it has. This process of noticing and registering facts is linked to the young child's natural curiosity. This is what drives her to look closely at more spiders to make sure that her information is accurate so that she can store this piece of information in her brain with confidence. The confidence gained in this way gives her the security that she has understood this new piece of knowledge and she will keep testing it until she knows without a shadow of a doubt that it is true. At this point she can be said to have developed *competence* in this particular piece of knowledge and her self-confidence will probably mean that she will enthusiastically tell her friends, family and key people '*Did you know that spiders have eight legs?*' She will rejoice in her new understanding and may well be motivated by this success to extend her understanding to other insects and perhaps compare the anatomy of other living things.

Understanding

Understanding is the eureka moment when pieces of a cognitive jigsaw fall into place. Most of the time young children know small pieces of information, as is appropriate for their level of cognitive development. As they mature and if they are helped to notice and concentrate on things that interest them, they will learn how to think logically and thus understand more about the world around them. Understanding requires deep-level thinking and very young children are perfectly able to think deeply about things that interest them. We will explore this further in Chapter 4. Ferre Leavers talks about what thinking deeply looks like. He describes children engaged deeply in thought as looking like '*fish in water*'[2]; in other words, completely at home in the midst of their learning. He also describes observable signs of this type of learning in terms of children's facial expressions, concentration levels and language. By observing the children we work with and know well, we will clearly be able to see, by watching them carefully, whether they are thinking at a deep enough level to be able to arrive at new levels of understanding.

Competence

This is the next part of the process. To be able to embed a new piece of understanding in the brain there must be opportunities to repeat that piece of learning to make very sure that it is absolutely accurate and can be relied upon next time it is needed. This then requires further opportunities to revisit the piece of new knowledge again and again until certainty of its validity is assured. This process is the same one that scientists use when making a new discovery. If scientists discover what is believed to be a new wonder drug, it will go through rigorous trials before reaching the market, just to make sure that it is consistently effective. This practice, or testing process, is particularly necessary with complex cognitive knowledge. Mathematics is one such area of learning where it is vital that children are not forced to move on to the next stage of understanding too quickly. If this happens, they may well have only an insecure grasp of an idea. For example, if they are hurried through 'counting on' (as in Snakes and Ladders or tens and units), they are likely to fail at the next step as this requires a secure understanding of these initial complex concepts. Competence is first about understanding and then about practising.

Theory into Practice

There are clear implications of both a practical and a pedagogical nature in the business of providing an environment where children are able to think, understand and become competent. To be in a place where thinking is encouraged, children will be finding things that arouse their curiosity so that they become involved in what is going on. Perhaps the practitioner has set up two water containers with a range of short, medium and long plastic tubes and jugs. Children will be encouraged to find out which length of tube is the most successful in transferring water from one container to the other. There will, of course, be mistakes along the way with water splashed on the floor but this is a part of the learning process and learning new concepts is rarely a tidy business. Once curiosity is aroused, children will spend a very long time, and concentrate deeply, on the task of transferring water from one container to the other. They will keep on trying, making mistakes along the way, but if practitioners support the learning and, crucially, allow the same learning to take place on a regular basis so that children can practise it, they will achieve competence and show genuine delight in their new understanding.

In this example the practical and the pedagogical are intertwined, as is so often the case with high-level learning. Practically, the mess is anticipated and allowed for in the planning process. Pedagogically, staff members are clear about what the children may be expected to learn from this activity so as to best support the learning. They are also clear that children will learn most effectively if given plenty of time and space and if they have a measure of control and independence about how they set about the task. Staff will recognise and value the characteristics of effective learning that they observe in this play, such as the concentration, the persistence and the enjoyment, whilst recognising that there will not be necessarily an end product such as a picture to take home or put on the wall at the end of the session. They will also be aware of the sensitivity of intervening, as too strong an emphasis on adult-directed learning goals are most likely to lessen children's enthusiasm and fewer characteristics of effective learning will then be seen. Some independence and control is vital for children to direct and monitor their own experiments so that they are able to concentrate and persist. In Chapter 8 we will be considering how daily routines support or constrain children's independence and control.

Observers of the water activity will note those children whose grasp of the way in which water travels indicates an understanding both of gravity and the nature of water. Staff will use this information to plan either a repeat of the activity or to add in complexity for those children who need further challenge. This type of play will provide rich opportunities to assess spoken language as children predict what might happen and try to guide the water flow. Also observable will be children's social confidence; who is in charge and who is interested but not yet confident enough to join in. This kind of provision gives rich opportunities for children to join it at a range of levels as described by Margaret Carr in her 'Learning Story Framework'. She notes children at five different observable points in their learning journeys[3]; all of which we will have observed as practitioners. This type of open-ended play, loosely structured with many potential learning opportunities, will cater for children who are:

- taking an interest
- being involved
- persisting with difficulty
- expressing an idea or feeling
- taking responsibility.

The theory

Having considered the practicalities of setting up a learning experience that is engaging and challenging, we need to ensure that the emotional environment of the setting is as conducive as the physical one.

Because this type of playful provision is open-ended and has a variety of levels at which it can be enjoyed, most children will feel that they can take part, or at least *'take an interest'*. Children need to feel secure and emotionally safe before committing themselves to an activity. They need to know the answers to questions such as *'What can I do here?'*, *'Does it matter if I make a mess?'*, *'How long have I got?'*, *'Will anyone help me if I get stuck?'*, *'Is there something I am meant to be doing or can I choose?'* If children can answer these questions to their own satisfaction they are much more likely to give the activity their best shot and thereafter display all the characteristics that suggest a high cognitive function.

Often children will be in possession of fragments of understanding about all manner of knowledge and we can see their thought processes as we observe them playing. We know, for example, that schematic play is, as Cathy Nutbrown so elegantly describes it, '*repeated patterns of play with threads of thinking running through them*'.[4] These threads gradually link together to form a new piece of knowledge or a new understanding about an aspect of life that until now had been uncertain. For the new knowledge to become secure and the child to become competent and assured of its validity, the experience must be available for the child to repeat time and time again. This process applies to concepts of science, such as the direction of water flow, but it applies just as equally to concepts involving relationships where a child needs to know who they can trust and who loves them reliably and consistently.

Our consistency as key people who are always engaged with our children and interested in them and their discoveries is central to their ability to learn successfully. We will all have experienced the emotional testing that young children engage in as they seek to be assured of an adult's constant affection. Once confirmed, this knowledge gives children the emotional security that they need to enter the uncertain world of new learning with its unforeseen implications and possible failures.

There are many examples of schematic play which are often compulsive and seemingly inexplicable. However, if we recognise schematic play for what it is, we may find it easier to provide supporting strategies for the child who, for example, is forever filling boxes and taking the contents home or covering her paintings with black paint! Schematic play is active in every sense of the word. It is active in that the child is physically enacting a concept or idea with which they are currently fascinated and it is evidence that the mind is actively wrestling with new and half-understood ideas. The fact that the child persists with their current investigation shows us that they are developing the habits of mind which will be useful all their lives. Among those habits are concentration, persistence and independence.

We have considered some of the aspects of mind that are necessary in the struggle for new knowledge and the effort that children willingly engage in to progress their understanding. Also involved in new learning is the satisfaction of enjoying and achieving one's goal.

Learning goals

It is sensible at this point to think about the motivation that drives children towards their learning goals. What is it that a child is trying to achieve by concentrating and persisting in a challenging activity? What exactly is it about being able to read or being able to sing a song or accurately kick a ball that is so motivating that children will, without any adult compulsion, return again and again to practise these difficult activities? There is in all of these skills a progression that children can see as they

Figure 3.1 *Reflecting delight in physical competence*

match their current level of ability with their performance when they began to try to master their chosen challenge and the acknowledged progress brings with it personal satisfaction and self-confidence. Singing, reading and ball skills have other benefits as well. Reading, for example, unlocks the mysteries of exciting stories, singing provides an uplifting feeling of co-operative, harmonious endeavour and good ball skills reflect the young child's delight in physical competence. Standards of achievement are registered by the young child and measured against past levels. The inevitable progress that comes with practise and encouragement from a key person provides the motivation to keep on trying and the rewards of deep satisfaction lead to genuine delight and sense of self-efficacy and pride.

This type of motivation is referred to as intrinsic and is thought to have an internal base. Intrinsic means that the motivation comes from within the mind of each person. The goals are about a child's own achievements and the knowledge that more effort will result in better progress comes from a mindset that is flexible and positive in outlook. These children are sometimes referred to as having a *'mastery orientation'*. They will have learned to enjoy a challenge in the knowledge that they can reach a positive outcome by concentrating, persisting and practising. They know that success is theirs for the taking if they put in the required effort. When things don't turn out quite as planned, this is seen as a necessary step along the way and not as confidence-sapping failure.

For these types of learners, rewards, which are often used by adults to encourage effort, are unnecessary because these children do not need them. They already know that effort brings results and the rewards of their successes are sufficient to drive them forwards. They do not need the approval of others as they are self-motivated and are unlikely to be interested in external standards or rewards. Less confident learners, however, do not have the same mindset and are less confident that their efforts will significantly change the outcome of what they are trying to achieve. These children are more reliant on what is known as external motivation; that is, the approval of others. They will depend on others to set their targets for them and will measure their success by how others rank their achievements. They will be less likely to recognise that success is in their control and will be less easy to convince that practice, concentration and persistence will bring the rewards they seek. In other words, these are children who do not feel that they have agency or control over their progress.

These attitudes persist into adulthood. How often do we hear someone saying *'I can't sing a note; I only sing in the bath'*. This is a sad reflection on what this person has been told very early on in life and is, by adulthood, accepted as fact. The real fact is that we all have a voice. Some are more tuneful than others, but with practice, sensitive teaching and the application of the same habits of mind that we recognise as valuable in young children, we would all have at least a serviceable voice which we could use to sing with others. The same is true of many other kinds of knowledge, the arts, literacy and mathematics perhaps being amongst the most obvious. Once adulthood is reached, our beliefs about ourselves as learners are much more fixed and so it behoves us as practitioners to encourage children to have a go at what captures their interest and to provide learning in suitably manageable chunks so that children can experience success regularly. This will in turn give them the confidence to believe in themselves as mastery learners.

Being a mastery learner involves having those dimensions of learning that were mentioned earlier. They are the habits of mind that are fundamental requirements to successful learning. As stated above, the Tickell Review describes them as:

1   Being involved and concentrating
2   Keeping on trying
3   Enjoying and achieving what they set out to do.

Resourcing mastery learning

Resources are the tools that each practitioner has at their disposal to make their vision a reality – the vision that the lead practitioner will have of how their setting will look and how it will enable children to learn in accordance with the practitioner's beliefs and understandings. Putting the vision into practice is often much harder than one might imagine because of the constraints we all will have experienced such as not enough space, an inexperienced workforce or lack of finance to buy the equipment that we would ideally love to have.

However, much can be achieved by taking a close look at our resources and making decisions about which elements are the most important. Recent research has showed that a well-trained workforce raises the quality of children's learning more than any other single factor. Often there is no money for off-site training and so the lead practitioner must find ways of explaining what is required to new staff members so that all the adults working in the setting understand why things happen the way they do. This will ensure that children receive consistent responses from all adults about such things as support for learning and behavioural expectations. In terms of resources, our staff is the most valuable asset we have and even the most committed early years team leader cannot realise their vision alone. One of the hardest, but most necessary, tasks that the lead practitioner has is to take the whole adult team in the right direction.

Possibly the next most valuable resource is that of time. This should be much easier to control but does require the adult team to recognise that deep-level thinking, concentrating and practising all take long and uninterrupted spells of time. The children described above, learning about the flow of water or carefully counting the number of legs on a spider, cannot complete these investigations to their satisfaction if they are continually interrupted for a snack time or other adult requirement. Timetables need to reflect the premise that if children are to be encouraged to become deeply involved in what they are learning, they need to know that they have as long as it takes or, at the very least, their creations can be safeguarded so that 'pack away time' does not contain the hidden message that children's efforts are temporary or of low value. Children who have thought deeply and struggled hard to gain a new understanding, construct a masterpiece with the bricks or in the workshop will not be tempted back to repeat the experience if their efforts are consistently met with the requirement to stop and dismantle.

Space

The space that practitioners allocate to playful learning gives out messages about its value. The domestic play area that is doomed to failure is the one that is poorly resourced and in situated in a dark corner where adults rarely go. Great care needs to be given to giving as much space as possible, particularly to those areas dedicated to imaginative play, as children's emotions will become engaged in high-level play and they will need to move around to fully express the ebb and flow of the game. The outside area comes into its own here as there is so much more freedom to spread out, hide and climb. These increased possibilities give children many more opportunities to think and imagine with greater complexity; indeed, practitioners will notice that some children get more deeply engaged in their play outside and this is partly because the richer environment and increased space provides more starting points and inspiration for their imagination.

Routines and organisation

When planning for thoughtful and productive learning it is vital to consider what equipment will be available for children to use and what rules will be in place. Equipment needs to be fit for purpose, not necessarily expensive but able to be used for a range of purposes, not just limited to a single function. If children can take their dolls, bricks or role-play equipment outside as their play requires, the quality of their thinking will be higher. Practitioners will be able to observe that children's conversations will be richer if they can use the equipment they need and, conversely, will be the poorer if denied that opportunity. Problems are likely to arise with concerns about keeping good-quality equipment clean so ways round this need to be considered such as providing outside dolls and inside dolls, the outside ones being allowed in areas where they might get muddy or covered in sand. These can be bought at very little expense from charity shops.

Routines

How settings organise their day will have a significant effect on the levels of thought seen in the children. If children can organise and manage their own activities it not only gives them a heightened sense of self-confidence but also frees the adults to talk to them about what they are learning rather than the lower-level managerial tasks that are a necessary part of everyday practice. For example, if children can select their own painting paper, put on their own aprons, choose their own paint, sign their own name and know where to put their paintings to dry, the adults are freed to talk about the content of the paintings and encourage children to talk about and reflect on what they are creating. This encourages a richer learning environment than adult/child discussions about doing up aprons or where pencils can be found. This seemingly small change of emphasis reaps huge dividends in terms of children's thought processes as they learn that adults are interested in what they know, feel and think about. Schools in general use many more managerial questions than these more thought-provoking ones and this tends to close down children's motivation to develop positive habits of mind and to think deeply about what they are doing.

Even the positioning of tables and chairs will affect how the play area is used. If there are barren empty spaces, children will tend to run around them in an unfocused way. If, however, there is balance between larger spaces with suggestions for their use such as dressing-up clothes or a stack of building blocks, and small enclosed areas that physically surround the children who enter them, there is enough variety to encourage different types of play. Children need areas where they can be expansive or thoughtful, alone or together, peaceful or noisy, experimental or competent.

To support the young child in active learning it is important, first, to be confident about the theory, about *why* active learning is the most successful way for children to learn, and then to implement this understanding with the practicalities.

In this chapter we have considered that both mind and body need to be active and engaged and we have thought through a range of ways to make this happen in the setting. We will find that, with theory and practice working hand in hand, we will have children who are, in the words of Margaret Carr, '*ready, willing and able*'.

Chapter 2 concentrated on children being 'ready'; this chapter has thought about them being 'willing'. Chapter 4 will consider the child who is 'able'.

Challenges and dilemmas

- How will you offer experiences to children that enable them to think deeply about what they are learning? Consider interactions and routines that support children making the struggle to understand. Offer opportunities for children to rehearse and practise their new learning so they are not moved on too quickly with insecure knowledge.

Creating and thinking critically

In order to be creative, a child needs not only the opportunity but also the capacity, the power to make a choice. *Christian Schiller*[1]

In previous chapters, emphasis has been placed on the groundwork that needs to be in place if children are going to be capable of higher-order thinking. For example, consideration has been given to the place that play has in enabling children actively and individually to explore their world. We have looked at the notion of emotional security and discussed the vital part it plays in enabling children to feel secure enough to experiment and try things out with confidence. We reasoned that independence and autonomy are building blocks for children's self-esteem and helps them feel that their individual views and choices are respected and valued. In this chapter it will be assumed that this groundwork is ongoing, the environment in which the child is learning is an enabling one both physically and emotionally. The words of Christian Schiller remind us, however, that there is one further step to be taken, that of giving the child the *skills* and the *power* to make choices for which she is then responsible. For a young child to be able to make purposeful choices that may have repercussions for herself and for others, she will need to be in possession of some sophisticated understandings about how the world functions and to be able to call on a range of skills that are both intellectual and practical.

Defining terms

To begin this chapter there will be an attempt to offer some working definitions of some of the terms connected with higher-order thinking and creativity. Following on will be some suggestions as to how these ideas might look in a setting.

Understanding versus knowledge

In order to be a creative and critical thinker, children need to be in an environment where they can develop their ability to understand basic concepts. As described in Chapter 3, children who are learning about the direction of the flow of water or about the nature of their relationship with their key person are engaged in a type of

Figure 4.1 *Having the power to make choices*

learning which can be thought of as 'understanding'. It gives a deep level of certainty and is very different from what schools are often dispensing which is 'knowledge'. Knowledge is often thought of as an academic discipline. It gives us information which is useful, such as the date of the Battle of Hastings. This is historical information which can be recalled and applied as and when it is needed but is not the same as deep-level understanding. Understanding a historical concept might be a growing awareness of the past, such as yesterday, or the future, such as tomorrow. A concept can be an easily tested scientific one, such as gravity (we understand all too well what will happen if we drop a valuable piece of pottery), or a complex one such as our relationship with our mother or carer. This latter concept is often less predictable as our concepts of motherhood will be affected by our experiences and will be less certain, whereas scientific concepts are often predictable and universal. To be able to think critically about complicated issues, children need to be able to base their emerging ideas on some certainties and some clear understandings. Because knowledge is not necessarily based on understanding and can be all too easily forgotten, it does not serve as such a useful basis on which to build future learning.

Symbolism and representation

The ability to use one object to stand for something else usually begins in a child's second year. It is at this point that a parent or carer may see a child push a teaspoon towards the mouth of a doll; this is a clear sign that the child has grasped the notion of the doll representing a baby and the child representing a parent. This is a hugely significant moment in a child's development because it is from this point on that they can imagine a world of their own creating. They are no longer bound by '*what is*' and can enter the world of '*what if?*' A toddler can been seen to wave '*bye-bye*' and if this happens at an appropriate moment, that is when people are leaving, it can be said to demonstrate an understanding of the symbol of waving to represent '*good-bye*'. Children's increasing abilities to use symbols to represent their experiences by role play, paintings, drawings, writing or numerical symbols gives children the gradual understanding that not only are there *things* all around to be learned about and played with but there are also *ideas* that can be learned about and played with too.

Playing with ideas and experiences is a key way in which children can practise what they are learning. Having begun to grasp the concept of, for example, letters as symbols of communication, the young child needs to find situations where they can rehearse what they have learned and to practise it regularly to verify its validity. Play is a most helpful way in which this can be accomplished. As an example of this, during a holiday in France we have a favourite cafe that is run by a young family. At the end of our meal the cafe owner presents us with our bill, closely followed by her five-year-old daughter who also presents us with a bill, beautifully written in her best emergent French handwriting! She has found an excellent play situation in which to practise her developing understanding about the purposes of writing together with the idea of being a waitress. She has interwoven these skills and ideas into a real-life scenario which makes the process even more meaningful for her. As this is France, the game is perfectly acceptable to all the customers who praise the writing skills of the tiny waitress with cheerful enthusiasm.

Theory of Mind and metacognition

The business of being able to understand the thoughts, beliefs and feelings of others and an ability to 'think about thinking' is an aspect of intelligence that, although it can be given a cognitive explanation, in reality has emotional and social implications for the developing child. Judy Dunn's work suggests that children often display their most logical reasoning in matters that are of great importance to them.[2] Consider the following scenario. Four-year-old Susie has been waking in the night, causing her parents and two-year-old brother to lose sleep as well. Having assured herself that there are probably no underlying causes, her mother decides to resort to a star chart which she puts up on the kitchen wall in an attempt to break Susie's waking habit. It is explained to Susie that she will be given a star to stick on her chart for each night that she sleeps without waking. When the chart is complete there will be a treat such as Susie's favourite chocolate bar. This arrangement, in itself, poses some difficulties for Susie. As with all habits, sleep patterns are hard to change. One might also ask how much control an individual, especially a young child, actually has over them. So Susie's chart gathers stars at a slow pace but eventually there is only one left to gain. Some interrupted nights go by without the opportunity to win the last elusive star. One morning Susie and her mother are in the supermarket which sells Susie's favourite chocolate. Susie devises an ingenious scheme and suggests to her mother that if she is really well behaved whilst the shopping proceeds she would deserve to win her last star and, as they are in the supermarket, could be rewarded instantly with the desired bar of chocolate!

This is truly a considerable cognitive feat. Susie and her mother have had different goals which have lead to this hi-jacking of the star chart. Susie's goal is the chocolate bar whereas her mother's goal is uninterrupted nights. This has caused a confusion which Susie has used to try to negotiate an outcome that suits her end goal rather than her mother's. She tries to substitute one type of good behaviour (being quiet in the supermarket) for another (staying asleep all night) which is an attractive option for her as, first, it is easier to achieve and, second, it brings immediate results. Susie needs to have a sophisticated insight into the workings of her mother's mind to be able to decide whether this scheme has a reasonable chance of success. She must predict possible outcomes which is a high-order cognitive function, whilst also using some emotional ploys such as pleading, otherwise known as '*pester power*', when her mother realises that she is in danger of being out-manoeuvred and refuses to negotiate. Interestingly, it is thought that children who have siblings are more able to interpret the meanings of interchanges between a range of people all with different personalities and agendas. David Wood describes these children as '*immersed in living soaps as they overhear, oversee and learn about the nature of human negotiations*'.[3]

Of course not all such mind games are negative. Many very young children will use their ability to understand their friends' thoughts and feelings to empathise and will comfort, companion and support their more vulnerable peers.

This is where play is so helpful. In their imaginative games children take on various roles as they step into the shoes of, say, the lonely giant or the wicked stepmother. Thus they have opportunities to experience not only the emotions of these characters but also to think about how their minds might operate. It is very likely that Susie practised, at least in her mind, if not in role play, the conversation with her mother including her mother's possible responses, before attempting the negotiation in the supermarket. Having a mind that is capable of insight, flexibility and negotiation helps children to develop their own original ideas and helps them to realise that they can make choices based on their own understandings. This is what is meant by metacognition and it leads to an understanding of how they can control and direct their own thoughts.

Metacognition is closely linked to the idea of Theory of Mind. Understanding how the minds of others may be working presupposes that children are quite capable of organising their own thinking. The much respected system known as '*Plan-Do-Review*', for example, is so constructed to encourage children to thoughtfully plan their activities and then reflect on them afterwards.[4] Thinking about the best way to do something in advance and being able to assess the success of your plans later leads to a habit of mind that discourages a haphazard approach in favour of a more organised one which is likely to lead to greater success.

Self-regulation is a part of the process of developing metacognition

Self-regulation has a range of meanings and is often thought to refer to children's ability to control their feelings and thus their behaviour. In this book, however, we are concentrating on how children's ability to self-regulate has a significant effect on their intellectual or cognitive ability. Self-regulation, in terms of children's cognitive development, is thought to help children to make meaning out of the information they receive, to be able to predict what might happen next and to find ways of solving problems. To paraphrase Christian Schiller's quote at the opening of this chapter,, to be creative, children need *to have the power to make choices*. The notion of children having power and making choices is often one that sits uncomfortably with some practitioners who feel that they must, at all times, be in charge.

How, we wonder, can such very young children make suitable choices? Will it matter if their choices result in failure? Is not the role of the teacher to provide correct answers and save children from making mistakes that might lead to a misconstruction of knowledge? These are interesting dilemmas and lie at the heart of our profession. The answers lead to an understanding of the differences between an environment where children are instructed, corrected and controlled and one where uncertainty is encouraged and creativity thrives. For children to be able to make choices they need to acquire some basic cognitive skills which can be taught in quite traditional ways. Let us consider some of the basic skills needed to become a creative and critical thinker.

Imitation

Much learning in young children comes from imitating the behaviour of those around them. Whilst not, in the strictest sense of the word, a skill, it is a process that exists in all children and one that we can encourage and foster. This process will give children access to meanings that they can explore and alter for their own purposes. Young children will attempt to replicate the actions of their carers – often after some time has elapsed indicating that memory is assisting the learning. What is thought of as imitation is, in fact, not quite as simplistic a process as straightforward replication. For a child to imitate an action they must first observe it accurately. It then has to be reconstructed in the child's mind. However, in the process of reconstructing the action, the child transforms it and takes ownership of it so that it becomes *their* version of what has been observed. Practitioners will often have noted the deep emotions invested in high-quality role play. Think, for example, of a group of children acting out a scene from *Jack and the Beanstalk* following a story session where the tale has been read to them. In their game the children experience genuine amazement at the rapid growth of the huge plant and a sense of anticipation and anxiety at the thought of climbing the beanstalk. This is followed by the fear of an encounter with the giant, the moral dilemma of stealing from him and the terror of the escape from the giant's castle. The children thus involved can hardly be thought of as pretending, so real is the game and so deeply engaged are the players. Cognitively, these children are operating at a high level as they make their own meanings from their playful experiences. This is not 'pretending' but 'being' and it is a process that enables significant experiment with complex emotional and factual concepts leading to an ability to feel confident with these, often abstract, ideas.

Memory

Babies and toddlers develop memory at a very early stage. If their lives are predictable they will be able to remember the song that their carer sang yesterday or the toy they found in their treasure basket that made a jangling sound. These happy experiences build into a bank of memories which provide stability and form a platform on which to extend their understandings of their world. Once a memory is stored it can be recalled and, at a later stage in development, altered to create something new. Think, for example, of the child asking for the same story repeatedly until the adult reading it is driven to exasperation! Developmentally this is a powerful process that the child needs to happen so that the complexities of the story, the characterisations and the sound of the language are all safely retained. It is then that the child can use this bank of knowledge and be creative. Perhaps he will act out the Gruffalo story using the deep voice for the main part and remembering the lilting pattern of the rhyming text. This is the *representation* that was discussed earlier. Later he will be able to use his knowledge to vary the story and make up his own version. Herein lies the beginning of creativity. There are many published alternative versions of well-known children's stories; perhaps the most well-known being *The Three Little Pigs*. *The Three Little Wolves and the Big Bad Pig*[5] is one such variation which relies on a child's familiarity with the original text and uses this to suggest an alternative. Once children understand how to vary the original story they will happily create their own versions of tales such as *Jack and the Beanstalk*, *The Enormous Turnip* and so on. Later on, children who are confident readers will relish books such as *Revolting Rhymes* which uses this same idea with poetry and they will copy the formula to create their own.

Memory encompasses every aspect of a child's life and is not, of course, confined to an understanding about how language works. A child will have a working memory of their relationships with their carers and will need to be assured of their consistent love, interest and encouragement if these experiments with creativity, some successful and some less so, are to be embarked upon.

Noticing

Children's innate curiosity about the world in which they find themselves is one of the most useful tools that practitioners have in helping children to gain the tools they will need to become effective learners. We considered, in Chapter 3, the girl whose attention had been brought to the eight legs on a spider and her subsequent insistence in checking any others that she spotted to validate her new discovery. This is a scientific skill and one that is easy to facilitate in the early years setting. This brings us back to the assertion that children's creativity will thrive in an environment where there is a range of possible outcomes to activities, where some uncertainty is encouraged and where the adults have attitudes that encourage flexible thinking. For children to develop their skills of noticing there must necessarily be things around them that are interesting enough to be noticed. If we think of the outside area, for example, I have recently seen some that are very safe with soft surfaces and all-weather grass. There are wheeled toys and bats with soft balls. There is a sand tray and some water to play with but children must not mix them together because of the mess this makes. If the weather is warm there is a rug and some of the less precious books, together with some chalks and some small-world play people with cars and a road mat. What, I wonder, is there to *notice* here? It seems that whilst there is little to challenge children's health and safety there is also little to challenge their intellect and to stimulate their creative potential.

A rich outdoor environment will contain places to dig, places to make camps and trails, things to climb and wildlife to study. It is this rich environment that will encourage the two-year-old to ask, in winter, '*Why are the trees empty?*' and the six-year-old to notice how his shadow is in different places at different times of the day. Each area of the setting must contain elements that are noteworthy and capable of triggering critical and creative thinking. As the EYFS practice guidance states, '*being creative involves the whole curriculum, not just the arts*'.[6]

Discussion

Discussion is the two-way conversation that takes place between interested and caring practitioners and the children in their care. An unsupportive learning environment that emphasises instruction, correction and control will find the practitioners asking direct and closed questions with children attempting to answer them. Any study of child development will tell us that this is not how children learn new knowledge. They learn by asking questions of carers who are ready to attempt to answer them. When we ask routine questions of children it is usually to fill in an assessment grid and its purpose is not to further children's understanding. What supports children to be critical and creative thinkers is the type of equal two-way conversation called '*sustained shared thinking*'.[7] This type of open-ended conversation encourages further cognitive skills such as those of questioning, prediction and reasoning. Much has been written about the value of open-ended discussion, flexible use of equipment and the need for children to have long spells of time to develop complex cognitive skills such as observing, reasoning and problem solving. Yet in today's fast-paced settings where much has to be achieved in the shortest length of time possible, good intentions are often sacrificed on the altar of expedience. Knowledge is quicker to impart than are the skills of effective learning. Information is easier to teach than are the more nebulous concepts of deep concentration, high self-esteem and an ability to be a self-regulating and critical thinker. However, it is interesting to note that, as this is being written (May 2012) a government select committee report on social mobility has just been published recommending an early years curriculum emphasising elements such as self-regulation and deferred gratification. Frank Field, a member of the parliamentary committee and a long-time crusader to improve the life chances of the most deprived children, stated that '*Anything we do after age five is just rescue work*'. Clearly, the sooner we start helping children to become creative, independent and critical thinkers the more effectively will their life chances expand.

The adult role

The only logical starting point for the practitioner who is determined to develop in children the characteristics of effective learning that they will need to lead fulfilling and self-directed lives is an understanding of and a confidence in the type of practice for which he or she is responsible. It is helpful at this stage to be very clear that, in the short term, this is not an easy option. The practitioner must wrestle with the types of questions we mentioned earlier. One such question to answer is '*How do I balance the control of the setting between the child and the adult so that children have adequate time and resources to learn deeply, independently and individually?*' Another key question is '*Do I believe that the process of learning is more important than the end product and how can I realistically give children the strategies they need to develop metacognitive skills?*' With skilful and specialised early years training which is based on a fundamental grasp of child development theory it is perfectly possible for new practitioners to base their everyday teaching on sound principles of good practice. The setting will appear as an enabling environment, both physically and emotionally, where the children are the most important people in it and where their wellbeing and achievements are nurtured. This will be a place where mistakes are a valuable part of the learning process, where there are interesting things to do and to think about and where time can be stretched to allow creations to be completed. The children fortunate enough to be a part of this setting will feel as if they belong, just as the adult staff do, and feel valued and respected. Sometimes the unpredictable happens and although routines and carers remain constant, there are often surprises. Uncertainty is welcomed as a challenge and adults will discuss and negotiate rather than direct. Negative behaviour is sensitively contained within agreed rules, and a system of working through such an event comes from a standpoint of attempting to understanding the reasons for it rather than a management of it. There is a belief that '*unreasonable behaviour is always reasonable from the point of view of the person doing it*'.[8] The community in which the setting sits is an integral part of the whole. Parents are recognised as their child's first and enduring educator and are asked to contribute their deep knowledge of their child so that the carers can learn from them. Family culture, habits, values and beliefs are respected and celebrated.

The above snapshot cannot hope to offer an in-depth description of an environment which supports children's developing metacognitive and creative skills but perhaps suggests a few starting points. Any practitioner who has travelled this path will know the huge rewards and the joy that results from watching very young children flourish as both their confidence and life skills develop.

Challenges and dilemmas

- Do your staff know the difference between concepts, that deep level of secure understanding of big ideas such as gravity or motherhood, and the ability to acquire new skills such as jumping, reading or singing? As a general rule, skills end in 'ing' and are visible. Both are valuable but very different.
- Give children imaginative play experiences in the knowledge that this will increase their exposure to, and understanding of, symbolism – a big cognitive function.

CHAPTER 5

Observing and assessing children's progress

Observing children is simply the best way there is of knowing where they are, where they have been and where they will go next. *Mary Jane Drummond*[1]

This chapter considers the EYFS requirement to '*Look, Listen and Note*' children's achievements. However, as well as assessing what children have learned, it also suggests that children's attitudes and learning skills should be noted and encouraged. This is in keeping with the purpose of this series which is to examine learning characteristics. It also links to the replacement EYFS profile which requires practitioners to assess these characteristics, in other words, to assess *how* children learn or their learning strategies, as well as their knowledge, or *what* they have learned. Ways of reflecting on practitioners' own teaching methods to encourage children's engagement, motivation and creativity will be outlined here, as will effective ways of observing practice and incorporating these observations into planning. There will be a deeper exploration of planning in Chapter 8 when we will consider how organisation and routines can be structured to support children's cognitive development.

The current EYFS places observation, planning and assessment in the strand named '*Enabling Environments*'. This positioning suggests that the observing, planning and assessing that happens on a daily basis is intended primarily for the benefit of the learners and that the process enables and supports children's progress. This assertion underpins this chapter and underlines the view that the prime purpose in watching and noting children's development is to ensure that what we say and do is working to each child's best advantage. So let us consider each of the major components in turn.

Looking

Observation is rightly placed at the heart of good early years practice. In reality it means watching and noticing. The quality of the noticing is similar to the noticing that we discussed in Chapter 4 when we were discussing how to develop the skills of creative and critical thinking in children. By watching our key children carefully we get to know them individually and thus we can begin to notice what

Figure 5.1 *Noticing achievements, difficulties and intentions*

is significant for their development and learning. We can notice not only their achievements and difficulties but also their intentions, their relationships, their preferences and their patterns of learning and behaviour.

Different types of observation are used for different purposes; the two most commonly used are participant, where the practitioner is engaged with the child or children being observed, and nonparticipant, where the practitioner stands back and makes a detailed record of what is seen and noticed. Children can be tracked to see which areas of the setting they frequent and they can be watched closely to gain information about their learning levels and styles. Whichever type of observation is used, it must be accurate, un-biased and focused. Only then can it be a valid tool which can be used to plan effectively for further learning and development. Observations that are valid in this way are one of the most valuable tools in the practitioner's possession as what they provide is *evidence* as opposed to *supposition*.

Often as an early years teacher, I would be visited by the teacher of the next class my children were moving on to. Suppositions would abound as comments about expected behaviour problems of a particular child were aired. This means that a professional's suppositions might affect the learning and developmental chances of that child. However, a focused and accurate observational record highlighting any particular difficulties and/or strengths of the child gives helpful information with which to plan for progress.

David, for example, was nearly five years old and about to move on to the reception class of a large primary school. He had an older brother, Christopher, who was a quick thinker, extroverted and popular. Christopher drew children to him, took responsibility for group learning and was a born leader. The reception-class teacher was delighted about David's imminent move into her class as children such as Christopher often provide positive role models for other children to aspire to. David had been in the nursery for five terms. He consistently did not talk to other children. He was usually alone and showed no move to make friends. He did not shun other children and would play alongside them but even when settled and confident in the setting he would not choose a companion or join in a group activity. The nursery team were concerned that David was overshadowed by his brother and that his timidity would prevent him from accessing the resources and help that he might need to progress.

A detailed observation was undertaken whereby David was tracked for a full nursery session and notes were made of his activities and conversations. Somewhat to the team's surprise, the observation revealed that David was achieving well. The current project, which was based on the story *The Owl Babies*, had appealed to his love of a good story and he spent over an hour in the workshop area making an owl from the cardboard rolls, feathers, paper, glue, scissors and string made available for the purpose. During the process he spoke to no one, but the observation revealed that this was because he was competent at the task he had set himself and needed no help. He cut the string and tied knots to attach the feather wings he had made and when the project was completed to his satisfaction he took it to his key person and whispered '*It's an owl for the night wall*'. He then demonstrated how he had succeeded in making the wings flap up and down so that the owl looked as if it was flying. He was confident in his use of all the equipment he needed, understood clearly the process he needed to go through to create an owl he would be satisfied with and his quietness was mainly due to intense concentration. In the discussion that followed it was clear that the staff had underestimated David's abilities and the new knowledge that they gained from the observation helped them to plan activities that would expand his range of interests and challenge him whilst respecting his quiet personality. By the time he left the nursery he would talk confidently, if still in a whisper, to his key person and occasionally to another child and had a better range of communication skills. His next teacher knew what to expect and planned accordingly for this quiet, yet rewarding, individual.

Listening

Listening, in the context of gathering information about how children are progressing, is sometimes known as 'seeing and understanding'. Sometimes it is called 'active listening' and both these phrases are helpful in describing the particular type of listening that provides information. Take the example of David whose flying owl was described above. When he took it to show his key person there were two possible responses she could have made; both could be called 'listening'. '*That's lovely, David, go and put it on the shelf*' is one possible response. It acknowledges, but is quite dismissive; the hidden message here is that the adult needs to get this creation dispatched to its correct place with a minimum amount of time and effort. Another possible response is '*Your owl flies beautifully, how did you get the wings to stick so well?*' This response could be called active listening as it is not only a genuinely enthusiastic response but is active in that there is a follow-up question that fulfils three important functions. First, the adult's genuine delight is registered and David's self-esteem rises accordingly. Second, there is a gentle attempt to draw David out a little, to expand his conversation skills. Third, the practitioner chooses her question carefully so that she asks a question he can answer; it is about the process he went through in the construction of his owl. The sort of '*what came first?*' and '*how did you do the next bit?*' type of questions are open-ended and they promote reflection and prompt memory.

This type of conversation can be thought of as helping David to 'represent' the owl-making experience. We considered the cognitive function of representing in Chapter 4 and its value in embedding ideas and knowledge securely in the brain. Here David is being gently encouraged to re-present his creative experience and, should his key person judge that it is appropriate, she might go on to ask '*And where is your owl flying to?*' which would give David an opportunity to expand his thinking into the imaginative realm as well as the technical one. This process is one that will take David's thinking to a higher level and challenge his intellectual abilities whilst remaining in a safe emotional context. In their book *First Hand Experience: What Matters to Children*,[2] the authors explain that the Chinese symbol for listening is made up of four different characters, all of which are involved in the function of listening. They are the ear, the eye, the brain and the heart, all of which were clearly involved in the example of David's conversation with his key person about his flying owl.

These authors also propose a list of what worthwhile listening means; here are a few examples:

- taking it slowly
- asking questions as well as answering them
- listening to yourself as you ask the questions
- listening to everybody's ideas
- listening to their meanings
- listening to debate and discussion

- listening to complaints
- listening with an open heart.

In her book *Listening to Four Year Olds*[3] Jacqui Cousins devotes an entire book to listening *'with an open heart'* to young children in a range of settings and she writes evocatively of the very strong feelings children have about the best and worst aspects of their school experiences. One of children's least favourite aspects of school life was the fast pace at which everything seemed to rush along, replicating many children's experience at home. Worthwhile listening, we are reminded, means 'taking it slowly'.

Worthwhile listening is central to the following aspects of children's cognitive development:

- The idea that worthwhile listening requires time is a key understanding in raising children's cognitive levels, as deep thoughtful activities and conversations cannot happen in the blink of an eye. They take time to nurture, evolve and mature.
- Worthwhile listening gives the practitioner the opportunity to engage in 'sustained shared thinking' with children which is key to the process of moving their thinking forward. This open-ended style of thinking and talking helps practitioners to understand not only what children know but also what their strategies are for finding things out. Evidence can be gained as to whether the child is, for example, noticing, persisting and concentrating. Kathy Sylva suggests that these kinds of preschool experiences *'put in motion a virtuous cycle of learning orientation'*.[4] This 'virtuous cycle', she continues, will stand children in good stead at school entry. In other words, good practice like this will help children to develop a positive disposition towards learning and to gather together the characteristics they need to become effective learners. (We will discuss this idea further in Chapter 9 when thinking about school readiness.)
- Worthwhile listening also enables adults to ensure that children are accessing the curriculum at a deep level. Bernadette Duffy writes, *'we need to be aware of the importance of ensuring that children are able to deepen their understanding'*.[5] Sometimes, in the effort to provide a broad and balanced set of learning experiences, we forget that, as Evangelou et al. remind us, *'Effective learning'* is thought to be learning that engages the child at a deep enough level to hold the child's interest at the edge of their understanding thus motivating them to learn more. *'It is important to aim at depth and not breadth.'*[6] Worthwhile listening to children's communications helps us to move them on to the next step in their thinking as, by listening to them, we are able to better understand their intentions and their meanings.
- In summary, children's thoughts, ideas and feelings are always important and it is only by listening to them that we can find out what they are. The revised EYFS proposes that, to get the best from children, practitioners should interact

with children by '*modelling, demonstrating and questioning*'.[7] I would like to suggest an addition to this list, that of listening.

Noting

Noting, or recording, what we have discovered about children's progress is not a stand-alone activity. The worst mistake we can make is to take notes on children and then add them to a folder that goes into a filing cabinet, never to be seen again.

One way or another, noting, or assessment to give it a more formal name, has to fit within a cycle of observation, analysis, planning and reflection. There are several ways of doing this, one of the best known is the New Zealand system called 'the Four D's of assessment'.

> Describing comes first, this is describing what has been seen or heard.
> Next comes discussing, where findings are discussed with the adult team.
> Following this comes documenting, or noting what has been discussed.
> Lastly comes deciding, or planning what should be provided in the setting as a result of the knowledge gained.

EYFS card 3.1 is clear in stating that anything that is planned for the Foundation Stage setting must follow the same pattern. It states, '*observe, analyse, and use what you have found out about the children in your group so that you plan for the next steps in the learning*'. This is similar to Mary Jane Drummond's assertion that assessment is '*the ways in which, in our everyday practice, we observe children's learning, strive to understand it and then put our understanding to good use*'.[8] This sounds reasonable and straightforward enough and yet, when I am training practitioners, the practicalities of assessment cause far more anxiety than any other aspect of practice.

The main complaint is that assessment is too onerous and that some local authorities are requiring statistics that can be used to total up scores to submit to government so that national figures can be assessed and improvement targets achieved. It should be clear that this type of assessment aims to assess the quality of provision whereas what practitioners are trying to assess is children's progress. These are two very different aims; both have their purpose but have become, in my view, confusingly intertwined. Dame Tickell, in her review of the early years Foundation Stage, reflects practitioners' anxieties by remarking '*Many have spoken to me of the burdens they feel have been introduced, through paperwork, moderation and the inspection process.*' She discusses just this issue, of the different purposes of assessment, in paragraph 3.48 of her review, acknowledging the dilemma of needing national accountability for quality of practice and the need to reduce paperwork and inspection. She hopes to resolve this issue by reducing the number of early learning goals to 17 from the original 69.

My suggestion would be a more radical one: that the quality of provision should be inspected by an additional set of criteria alongside those used to assess children's progress. It is quite right that quality of provision is assessed but I would argue that early years quality provision has more to do with issues such as the level of practitioner qualifications and, in particular, their understanding of child development than whether children are achieving the early learning goals. In addition, the setting's relationship with families and carers and the emphasis that is placed on developmental aspects such as wellbeing, physical health and autonomy give a far clearer indication of the quality of the practice to be found in a setting. It is worth noting that children in settings where these aspects are prioritised are more likely to be progressing well towards the early learning goals too.

The statutory requirements regarding assessment are as follows:

- Practitioners should make systematic observations and assessments of each child's achievements, interest and learning styles.
- They should use these observations and assessments to identify learning priorities and plan relevant and motivating experiences for each child.
- They should match these observations to the early learning goals.
- Within the final year of the Foundation Stage each child will be assessed against the 13 scales of the EYFS profile. These judgements should be made from *observation of consistent independent behaviour, predominantly children's self-initiated activities.*[9]

The words in italics reinforce the 'enabling' aspect of the assessment process: that assessments are to be made from observations of children engaged in play. There are no requirements that practitioners make numerical assessments when planning for children's progress (known as formative assessment), or when using the profiling documentation for assessment at the end of the Foundation Stage (known as summative assessment). Most parents much prefer a verbal account of their child's progress, written by their child's key person who knows them well and whose judgement parents will trust. In this type of summative assessment the child can be invited to contribute. These contributions might include photos taken whilst in the setting, and their hope and fears about moving to a new class.

The daily ongoing, or formative, assessment is the one that plays the largest role in ensuring that each child is being offered the experiences that will best enable them to progress. It may be helpful to have some underpinning principles of formative assessment in the Foundation Stage as these will provide a framework within which to set up systems to ensure regular and useful information gathering.

Formative assessment in the Foundation Stage:

- is rooted in observations of what children say and do
- occurs in contexts with which children are familiar
- is based on what children can do rather than what children cannot do
- recognises that children learn from activities which they are motivated to choose for themselves
- acknowledges that children's achievements are affected by their relationships with adults and peers

- is rooted in principles of equality of opportunity and in the celebration of diversity.

Having established a framework of principles it is then sensible to ask ourselves the following practical questions:

1 *What* is noteworthy?
2 *How* to make assessments?
3 *Who* should assess?

The short answer to the question 'What is noteworthy?' is that anything that is significant for the child is noteworthy. Jennie Lindon reminds us that '*Formative assessment is sometimes called "continuous" in the EYFS pack. This word may explain why some practitioners believe they have to be writing on a constant, non-stop basis. You cannot, nor are you expected to, write down everything, nor to amass piles of evidence that have no genuine pay-off for individual children and their enjoyment of time with you.*'[10] Other writers refer to formative assessment as 'catching glimpses' of what is significant for a particular child. No one will be able to assess 'continuously', nor are they meant to. What is continuous is the noticing, the awareness and the alertness to any significant achievement or difficulty that a child demonstrates.

In terms of cognitive development there are two main aspects that need noting: one is contained within the curriculum, that is literacy, numerical, scientific skills and understandings; and the other is much broader and concerns the learning styles of children. There is some conflict here which, it is hoped, will diminish with the introduction of the revised Early Years Foundation Stage with its emphasis on the characteristics of effective learning.

Pascal and Bertram warn that '*what has become important to governments is that which is most readily measurable and that which is measurable has therefore become the most important*'.[11] What is most readily measurable is curriculum based such as reading scores and counting skills whereas learning characteristics are more fundamental to children's success but are less easy to quantify. Christopher Ball refers to these characteristics by stating '*No-one learns effectively without motivation, social skills and self-confidence*'[12] and follows this with the assertion that embedding these attributes into young children is the prime function of early years settings. Reflecting these ideas are the characteristics of effective learning that will be assessed in the revised EYFS as practitioners note children's progress in 'playing and exploring', 'active learning' and 'creating and thinking critically'. The practical organisation and the strategies that will support practitioners to assess these will be fully discussed in Chapter 8.

The process of making formative assessments (the 'how') should be informed by the above extract from Jennie Lindon. The key is not to amass piles of paperwork that have no pay-off for individual children. It is a matter of catching glimpses and making brief comments about what has been seen or heard on Post-it notes. Helpful evidence can be gathered by the conversations had with colleagues, the photographs taken by staff or children, the tangible evidence collected, such as drawings and writings, and regular liaison with families. These notes are sometimes called 'jottings' and are informal and brief. They do, however, feed into regular staff reviews where time is set aside to talk about individual children and to feed this information into short- or medium-term planning. Sometimes these jottings accumulate to give a story of a child's learning and are, in fact, called 'learning stories'. The New Zealand curriculum (Te Whariki) use these stories as their major method of assessment and progress is noted as each child's learning story becomes deeper and more complex as their understanding of the world and their place in it increases.

Central to assessing the effective characteristics of effective learning is the provision of an environment which supports their development. As card 4.3 of the EYFS document reminds us, '*It is difficult for children to make creative connections when colouring in a worksheet or making a Diwali card just like everyone else's.*' For the purposes of this chapter, it becomes clear that it is also difficult to assess children's ability to be creative, active or playful when engaged on these types of activities.

The importance of the quality of the learning environment cannot be over stressed. For children to be able to demonstrate their positive dispositions to learning, such as '*being willing to have a go*' or '*choosing ways to do things and finding new ways*' there have to be thought-provoking and interesting things to 'have a go' at. There must be challenging experiences for children to 'find new ways' (or problem solve) about. The struggle that is involved in investing time, cognitive effort (thought) and emotional resources (risking failure) must be worthwhile.

Who should assess children? The answer to this is that everyone who is important to the child should have a voice, including the child. The key people with valuable insights into children's progress are parents, carers, other professionals and the setting's team, especially the child's key person. The day-to-day formative notes are usually made by a combination of a child's key person and the child's family. By sharing records with families a much fuller and richer picture can be built up. If families are aware of what is being looked for, or what the child's next steps might be, a regular conversation can be engaged in whereby families feel that they are not only contributing to their child's assessment but contributing to their progress too. It is important to remember at this point that it is not only children's cognitive development that is being noted and assessed and that families have a huge contribution to make in supporting emotional, physical and social aspects of development as well.

Assessment, professionally and sensitively undertaken, provides secure evidence on which to plan for future learning. It gives practitioners the ultimate confidence that they are correct in what they are planning and the results offer parents reassurance that the setting staff know and understand their child well. Based on valid observations and on regular discussions with the adult team the evidence gathered gives accurate (if sometimes unexpected) information with which to chart progress and to take appropriate action. High-quality observation and assessment are the building blocks of good practice but excessive and mountainous paperwork is quite the opposite. It is demoralising, purposeless and a poor use of practitioners' time. A wise head teacher once told me, '*You cannot fatten a pig by weighing it*'.

Challenges and dilemmas

- Ensure that staff observe and assess children's attitudes and dispositions to learning as well as what they know they can do (Concepts and skills).
- Practise worthwhile listening by thinking of responses to children's creative offerings that give them opportunities to reflect on what they have created thoughtfully. How you respond can also help to deepen understanding and extend knowledge.

CHAPTER 6

Partnerships with parents and community

What is learned does not reside just in the head of the learner. The world we are interested in is not just the world of the individual, it is the world of the individual in relation to people, places and things.[1]

In considering the development of the young child, two beliefs run through this chapter. One is that the child is not isolated. We often talk of individualised learning and understand that each child constructs their own picture of the world depending on their own particular experience of it. However, no concept is learned in a vacuum and it is a truism that a child's interpretation of every new feeling, idea or concept they encounter is coloured by their experience of their life so far. All young children's learning can be said to be socially mediated. For the very young child those mediations are most likely to have been encountered within the family. Just as powerful is the influence of the immediate community in which the child is situated and which has its own particular cultural and moral ideology.

The second premise on which this chapter is based follows on from the first. It makes great sense for practitioners to find out about the type of learning to which the child has been exposed at home and to build on this in the Foundation Stage. This is because parents know their children best and know their interests and styles of learning. It makes little sense, and indeed can be very damaging, to introduce different styles of learning than those that have already proved to be very successful in the child's earliest years. Both these ideas will be explored further.

The child in context

Each child is born into a family unit of some kind. Today, these units vary enormously in structure. One of the key findings from the Early Years Learning and Development Literature Review was that *'Children thrive in warm, positive relationships characterised by contingent response'*.[2] The first part of the quotation is perhaps not a new idea, but the second part, the value of the *'contingent response'*, or the value of an adult responding to a child's initiation, is a finding from neuroscience that allows us to pinpoint the nature of the interchange between adult and child that furthers development. Most obviously, a child's emotional and social development is hugely affected by these early intimate relationships and we now know that '*continued raised cortisol levels in the brain caused by a failure to maintain effective relationships can be hazardous to the brain*'.[3] If the brain's function is impaired this will affect the cognitive process as well as the emotional process. We know that the characteristics of effective learning contain elements which will be hard for a child to access if the basic need, to be thought of as loveable, is unfulfilled. Most children who are able to risk failure by trying out something new or concentrate for a long period of time on a complex new piece of learning have, at their core, a knowledge that, even if they fail, they will still be loved and that they are a worthwhile enough person to be able to master a new piece of learning if they work hard enough at it. These characteristics are more likely to be seen in children who have been exposed to these reciprocal and contingent responses in the home right from birth.

Governments make much of the notion that it is better for a child to be raised in a traditional family with two married parents, one of each gender, but recent research tells us that the composition of a particular family is not the most important issue. It is the *nature* of the intimate family relationships which have such a deep impact on the young child and not its structure. Families are now known to provide not only an emotional influence but an intellectual one too, as many of children's patterns of learning are laid down at this early stage in life when they are predominantly with their family. These early experiences that children have will affect the architecture, or physical structure, of their brains and repeated exposure to either reaffirming or negative experiences with carers will make a huge difference to how they see themselves as effective learners.

One of the strengths of the Peers Early Education Project (PEEP), a literacy intervention project based in Oxford, is the underpinning assertion that it is not *who you are* as a parent that enables your children to be effective learners, but *what you do* that makes a difference. This understanding has enabled families of all types to understand that by offering warm, reciprocal relationships, recognising children's achievements and modelling appropriate behaviours, they significantly improve their children's life chances. Thus the process of *contingent response* can be taught and children's cognitive function, as well as their emotional and social functions, will be enriched. It is precisely because this emotionally reciprocal type of relationship is so vital to successful learning that each child in the Foundation Stage is entitled to a key person. The EYFS commitment of 'Positive Relationships' states that a key person '*gives children the reassurance to feel safe and cared for*', recognising that without those feelings of emotional safety and belonging that a key person gives, a child's chances of becoming a confident learner are significantly reduced.

Learning that one is lovable is entirely dependent on very early experiences with one's main carer. As repeated experiences lay down patterns of understanding long before conscious memory is in place, these patterns are necessarily based on feelings. As Maria Robinson states, '*Our initial feeling responses will help attract and maintain or lose our attention and so will influence what we remember*'.[4] She goes on to

Figure 6.1 *Learning that one is lovable is dependent on early experiences*

assert that stress impacts on our ability to remember and therefore to learn, thus suggesting an intertwining of emotional and cognitive development from the very beginning of life. This may perhaps be a similar sort of stress to that which many of us recall from primary-school days when we were asked to perform a mental arithmetic sum or to recite a multiplication table, only to discover that our mind had gone blank! Speaking from experience here, I can confirm that this can lead to a long-term inability to function mathematically which is linked to a lack of confidence rather than an innate lack of mathematical ability.

The family, then, is the most powerful influence on the child. Each family, in its turn, is not isolated but a part of a community which will have a range of racial, cultural and religious identities. These ideas will impinge on the young child whose developing view of their world will be, as we suggested earlier, socially mediated by the family and wider community. These powerful early experiences that we all have within our family and community do not simply affect our brains, they actually change who we are. So the person we become is a direct result of these early influences.

There are several fundamental beliefs about children's home learning that have changed in the last fifty years, all of which have influenced the way that teaching in the early years has been conducted. First, it is now acknowledged that the baby's and young child's brain grows at its fastest rate between birth and six years. Thus it follows that, far from knowing very little as a young child, we now know that children learn a huge amount about concepts, skills and relationships whilst in their family. Second, we know that the type of learning they have experienced is very successful as it is tailored to the individual child's way of learning and social environment. Research by Tizzard and Hughes showed, for example, that the conversations between young working-class girls and their mothers were far richer and more complex that those they had at school with their teachers.[5] Third, we have become more sensitive to the view stated in the opening quotation of this chapter that a child comes to our setting, not as an isolated individual but in a context of 'people, places and things' that make each child unique. This tightly woven web which usually supports, yet occasionally constrains, a child is indivisible from the child and needs to be understood and respected as such.

It is important to understand what it is about the learning that children experience at home that is so effective. Consider the following example:

> Josh who is five and Sally, three, are cooking biscuits with their mother. This is a common activity and can be easily imagined. There are ingredients to be sorted, weighed and mixed, dough to be rolled and shaped cutters to be manipulated. Once placed on the baking tray the biscuits need to be timed in the oven before being removed and cooled. They are then divided between an assortment of dolls, family members and friends whilst the remainder go in the tin to be eaten another day. The whole experience is described in great detail to any family members who can be persuaded to listen and possibly the story of The Gingerbread Man is read at bedtime that evening.

Looking at this activity through a formal learning perspective it is perfectly possible to catch glimpses of many areas of the curriculum. There is mathematics as ingredients are weighed out and as biscuits are checked out against numbers of recipients. There is science as the biscuits change consistency during mixing and cooking. There is communication and language as instructions and conversations take place and there is social development as turns are taken and patience is encouraged. Also in evidence are some of the characteristics of effective learning as Josh and Sally find out what it feels like to mix and then knead the biscuit dough. They display motivation and persistence as the biscuit dough breaks up and they need to roll it out again to match their dough shape to the cutter. They experience deep satisfaction from a job well done as the biscuits emerge smelling delicious and they then choose how to complete their game as they make a tea party for their dolls.

One powerful aspect of this as a learning experience is not so much that the curriculum has been 'taught' through this cooking activity but that it has happened in a holistic, playful way with never a mention of science, language, maths or social development. One of the major advantages that this type of activity has over more formal, subject-based learning is that young children need to have their learning embedded in their own experiences. To develop cognitively, activities have to make sense to the child. It can be said that a child's only job is to make sense of the world and to gain an ever-increasing level of understanding of how things function. For the child it makes sense to count out how many dolls there are and how many biscuits will be needed to feed them. There is much less sense to be made of an activity where a practitioner asks a child to count out a number of objects in the setting. This latter activity seems to the child to have no obvious sense. The resulting learning will be less securely embedded in the brain and concentration will flag as the exercise appears pointless. Research by Margaret Donaldson in 1978 demonstrated just this phenomenon as she showed that children could understand complex concepts if they were embedded in everyday playful contexts whereas if the same concepts were presented in a de-contextualised way, such as some of Piaget's experiments exploring egocentricity, children did not understand what the meaning of the tests were and failed them.[6]

Another powerful aspect of this type of home learning is the role of Josh and Sally's mother. Munn and Schaffer found that the home environment can be '*highly adaptive to children's cognitive functioning*' because parents are often very sensitive to their children's abilities and preferences and are able to support and scaffold their children's emerging understandings.[7] The parent as teacher is unlikely to be didactic or instructional but is likely to be closer to the co-constructional model where an outcome is often flexible and negotiations are encouraged. The recently published government select committee interim report on social mobility suggests that if parents are encouraged to spend time with their children in just these kinds of informal scenarios, children will be able to gain key characteristics of effective learning such as delayed gratification and self-control.[8] This co-constructional model of interaction is a key feature of both the infant and toddler schools in Reggio Emilia and the Effective Provision of Pre-School Education (EPPE) report. We are back to the sort of interaction that supports what the EPPE report calls '*Sustained Shared Thinking*' – an equal, two-way conversation where each person's contribution has equal value and there is the possibility of the critical thinking we explored in Chapter 4. Cognitively, this is an approach that encourages the children's viewpoints, thus valuing their contribution and offers the possibility for more complex types of thought. For example, Sally and Josh's mum may well encourage the children to search out one more space to fit their cutter into the dough for another biscuit. She will not necessarily point out where the space is but support them as they search for it. There may be two options that the children have to discuss and they may choose a solution that their mother would not have thought the best one. She may, however, let them make their own decision or she may suggest that their reasoning is flawed. Either way, she is sensitive to their learning needs and can offer her support at just the optimum point necessary to take their understanding to another level. Lev Vygotsky called this point the 'zone of proximal development' and it is thought to be one of the most valuable type of adult interactions in promoting cognitive growth. In fact, so influential is this type of home learning that Melhuish et al. rated it as equal in status to the mother's level of qualification which is considered as a key indicator of children's likely cognitive progress, stating unequivocally that *'what parents do* is more important than *who they are'*.[9]

To summarise, these are some of the main reasons why parents are such successful educators of their children:

- parents love and care about their children
- parents operate in the real world rather than the more formal one of academic learning
- parents are often in a one-to-one situation with their child
- parents usually respond to rather than initiate learning.

Partnership with families

Melhuish et al. note that however rich the home learning environment is, the sole responsibility for early learning must not fall on families alone. Wheeler, Conner and Goodwin reiterate this by stating *'It is not surprising that the most effective early years settings and schools have been found to work closely with parents'*.[10]

'Working closely with parents' must qualify as one of most complex aspects of every practitioner's role. It is a phrase that trips so easily off the tongue and many settings believe that they are fulfilling this requirement. It is worthwhile exploring the nature of parental relationships rather more deeply here because if it is as crucial as the research suggests, we must be quite certain that the type of partnership offered is one that parents feel is appropriate for them.

Parent's involvement in learning

Many parents are aware of the role they can play in their children's cognitive development and are regular visitors to their child's setting, attending meetings to do with children's learning and completing home/setting records of books read and activities completed. These parents will volunteer to read stories, bake, accompany outings and be engaged in the full range of the setting's provision. They are likely to be confident, in an environment where learning is highly valued, and to be comfortable in the company of large numbers of small children. They will understand that there is a philosophy underpinning the practice and will be eager to understand it and the principles that it enshrines. They will also have to be willing to undertake the necessary checks currently needed to be in the company of young children and to be able to give consistent amounts of time on a voluntary basis. In my experience there are not many parents able or willing to offer support at such a level. It is probably unreasonable to expect such a commitment and consequently it is always a struggle to encourage enough parents to get involved in this way. However, the few such parents that a setting may have gained provide not only a source of enormous practical support but also act as invaluable links to other parents in the community. These are the parents who understand why the setting functions as it does and act as valuable advocates to other parents, assuring the community that the practice is good and the learning effective. They see that children are happy and engaged, as are the members of staff. There is a feeling of belonging and wellbeing, of confidence, achievement, curiosity and co-operation. The general message here is that parents must be encouraged to become as closely connected to the setting as is reasonably possible because it is through this regular and often informal contact that a truly joint and equal partnership can flourish.

Other ways of involvement

The majority of parents are not, for a variety of reasons, going to be involved in their child's setting on an everyday basis. Practitioners need to think creatively about a range of ways to make and keep contact with parents who lead busy lives and not make the assumption that any one method of partnership is better than another. Some parents are happy to accompany children and staff on outings; others to make role-play clothes. Some will be happy organising the summer barbeque whilst others may contribute spare paper, collect boxes for the workshop or take the guinea pigs home for the weekend. All these ways of building a genuine friendship offer benefits for both the child and the setting and in the course of making these arrangements genuine opportunities arise for informal conversations which help practitioners to get to know their families better and the parents to feel acknowledged and valued.

To be supportive of a setting in a way that increases their child's cognitive development, parents do not need to understand the latest ways of teaching number bonds or the theory behind synthetic phonics. Parents sometimes worry that methods of learning change so frequently that their own ways of, say learning to read or count, will be out of date and therefore confusing for their child. This is to misunderstand the nature of support that is required to encourage their children's learning. To be most effective, a parent needs the following attributes:

- to be interested in what their children tell them about the setting
- to have time to share books and other experiences that happen within the setting
- to be supportive of the setting's philosophy.

What settings can do

To promote genuine partnership, information must flow in both directions, both from and to parents. Settings have a range of ways of informing parents both about the philosophy that underpins the practice and the everyday mechanics of the organisation. Each of these aspects of the setting is as important as the other as they impact on each other and are interdependent. For example, the fact that each child needs to be able to recognise their own coat is linked to the philosophy that independence is encouraged and children may be expected to find their coat, with help if necessary of course. Parents need to understand that every aspect of the setting's organisation supports the philosophy so that they can support it too. We will consider these particular issues in more detail in Chapter 8.

A brochure gives an opportunity for the setting to make clear statements of its beliefs as well as details of everyday organisation. Care should be taken to ensure that it is accessible to the full range of families so that the whole community feels a sense of belonging and of being valued. This is a valuable way settings can ensure that all families develop an interest in the setting and its philosophy, find the time to read to their child and take an interest in their child's experiences at the setting.

Settings can organise workshops sessions which cover a range of topics. A session on learning through play helps parents understand how vital it is to present new learning in an informal way and may prevent '*the dangers of over-teaching on the parents' part*'[11] which can lead to the stress that hinders rather than encourages new learning. A particularly useful session that I used to hold was about risk and resilience. Parents often worry about the risks involved in the first-hand experiences that their children will meet and worry that they are not yet confident enough to voice their concerns. This session gives parents the opportunity to ask questions about how risk is managed and practitioners have the opportunity to explain how managed risks promote cognitive growth, creativity and critical thinking. This particular issue will also be explored in more detail in Chapter 8.

Sometimes settings run a range of sessions on wider family issues such as parenting or behavioural matters. Sometimes there are opportunities to cook or to sew or to become more proficient at a language. During these times families can share expertise and get to know each other as well as learning more about how their children are being taught. The setting becomes a centre for the community which promotes a genuine feeling of belonging for the community of parents that the setting serves and sometimes provides a starting point for parents to consider working in early years settings themselves.

Learning from families

No setting can promote children's cognitive growth without a full understanding of the children in their care. There is no one better able to give exactly the information we need than parents. We need to ask both the questions that give us vital information, such as individual preferences and anxieties, as well as allowing parents to tell us what they feel is important that we should know about their children. After an initial questionnaire and conversation at the start of the association between family and setting, it must be made clear to parents how regular contact can be maintained. Settings must organise their systems so that parents can have informal conversations with their child's key person so that trust and information can be exchanged.

A genuine partnership with families is a clear indicator of a setting that is providing well for its children. One that has not worked at developing a good relationship with families will be unlikely to be able to maximise the opportunities available and thus to offer the very best care and education to all its children. It is true to say that the strengths of families and setting staff working together is a powerful model for progress and successful leaning.

Challenges and dilemmas

- Settings must put in place genuine two-way exchanges with parents. We are often very good at providing families with the information we think they need but not always so good at learning from them about their in-depth knowledge of their child.
- Staff need to understand deeply that contingent and reciprocal responsiveness is at the core of cognitive learning as well as social and emotional development. There needs to be a daily expression of professional love towards their key children to maximise progress.

CHAPTER 7

Thinking differently

> Children should be treated fairly regardless of race, religion or abilities. This applies no matter what they think or say; what type of family they come from; what languages they speak; what their parents do; whether they are boys or girls; whether they have a disability or whether they are rich or poor.[1]

Difference comes in many guises. Some differences are actual and are linked to physical, cognitive, social or behavioural disabilities or limitations. These differences sometimes give rise to what is called special educational needs. Other differences are perceptual. Perceptual differences might include people with a range of cultural or religious beliefs and backgrounds which appear to place them in a minority.

The notions of difference and minorities lie at the heart of this chapter as they have significant effects on cognitive processes. Some of the dominant ideas about how young children learn, and therefore how they are best taught, are helpful to understand. There are predominant ways of thinking about learning that currently have a huge influence on what our settings look like as well as the goals that practitioners are required to achieve. There will also be a consideration of difference as it applies to ways of learning, echoing the first of the EYFS themes and commitments, 'A Unique Child'. As card 1.1 reminds us, '*Babies and children develop in individual ways and at different rates*'. So let us consider some definitions.

Dominant thinking

Dominant thinking consists of ideas and practices that carry weight and influence and are therefore built into everyday practice. It is important at this point to recognise that these ideas are not necessarily universally accepted. An example might be that of developmental psychology which provides a particular context for early learning that relies heavily on a linear progression through a recognised set of stages and is thought to be universally applicable. The advantage of this pedagogy for governments is that it makes learning and development relatively tidy so that it can be assessed and thus regulated. More recently, however, different ideologies have come to the fore, mainly because, as Dahlberg, Moss and Pence so wisely state '*You cannot legislate for people's understanding*'.[2]

Learning and development are increasingly thought to be culturally bound and to be more organic than a linear shape might suggest. This pedagogy recognises that children do not learn in straight lines and that many factors influence their ability to learn. Some of these factors may be physical, such as poverty, and some of them may be cognitive and emotional, such as low self-esteem. The weaving together of the various elements that support or restrict children's ability to learn and develop need to be recognised by practitioners and then considered in their planning so that each child has the opportunity to thrive. One such example of just this kind of dilemma was in my early years setting where I had two sisters who had recently arrived from Thailand. Their English was at an early stage and their mother spoke very little English. The major difficulty that the staff had was in trying to persuade the two little girls to play, even with each other. It seemed that they could not connect what they thought of as 'school' with playing. Eventually, I found a translator who explained that these children would have experienced a much more formal style of schooling and that none of their family would have encountered the concept of learning through play. This is a classic example of a family meeting a dominant theory; except that, of course, that it was not dominant in the part of the world that they had left. As a family, they were certainly '*thinking differently*'.

Minorities

Leading on from the idea of dominant pedagogies is the idea of being part of a minority. The concept of 'us' means different things to different people but professionally it needs to mean everyone who is part of our setting.

In social-science research terms, the majority is thought to be the perspective of the white male in Western culture. It is here that the majority of the power, influence and wealth lies and it is from here that our current education agenda emanates. In England at the moment the power lies in the hands of those who require a tidy education system with easily definable targets and clear tables of measurement. This fits well with the pedagogy of developmental psychology with its linear progress and universal application. Following on from this pedagogy comes universal formulaic remedies for those children seen to be falling behind. One such remedy is synthetic phonics which is a technological and simplistic approach to a complex and multi-causal problem. Rather as a car can be fixed by replacing a broken part with a new one, a course of synthetic phonics, universally applied, is seen as the quick fix to the country's literacy crisis.

Given that the majority is thought to be the white, Western male, a very large proportion of the world's population can be seen to be outside this group and can therefore be categorised as the minority. Women, children, those of non-Western origin and those with differing abilities constitute by far the largest number of people but have substantially less influence over policy making. The influence of

Western culture, led by the huge financial, academic, cultural and technological prowess of the United States, has led to an unprecedented flow of ideology outwards into the rest of the world. This therefore suggests that its views and values are the norm and that anything different should be thought of as 'other'. Being thought of as other brings us back to the knotty question of who we consider as 'us'.

Dispositions to learn

In cognitive terms, the disposition to learn is, as Lillian Katz explains, a '*tendency to exhibit frequently, consciously, and voluntarily, a pattern of behaviour directed to a broad goal*'.[3] It is this tendency that we need to explore as it is this that enables children to thrive and learn. A significant part of this tendency is the belief that one is valued and loved and that one belongs to the community of learners that one has joined. Imagine joining an adult evening class in French conversation, for example, and realising that everyone else has been attending for some years, they know each other well and are far advanced in their conversation skills. This realisation does not help the feeling of being a part of the group; in other words, you do not share the 'us' feeling and you feel in a minority. It often takes a long while for this to change and the change depends on a variety of factors such as your social skills, the philosophy of the group in welcoming newcomers and the skill of the group leader in structuring the learning.

In a setting, too, a new child will feel little disposition to learn if they feel an outsider and that the efforts they make will not be valued. It needs a sensitive practitioner to recognise that the 'other' child may need gentle encouragement and a secure emotional attachment to foster the warmth and consistent friendship that will encourage the '*repeated pattern of behaviour*' that leads to a positive disposition to learning.

Dispositions have two elements, the emotional and the cognitive. The desire to try something new requires both courage and a degree of self-confidence. Self-confidence comes from a secure knowledge that one is a worthwhile being and that, by trying really hard, something difficult can be achieved. The belief that our effort is likely to be effective and that we can effect change is known as an *internal* locus of control. We all know children who see something difficult as an exciting challenge and know with certainty that they stand a good chance of succeeding at whatever they apply themselves to. These children have what is often called a mastery attitude to learning which Carole Dweck researched in depth.[4] This type of learner, she found, is self-motivated and self-regulated and capable of the complex critical thinking and metacognition that were discussed in Chapter 4. The other type of learner is referred to as 'helpless' in that they consider someone else to be in control of their ability to learn; they have an *external* locus of control. The motivation for this learner in making an effort is to gain the approval of another rather than the intrinsic pleasure to be found in the challenge of the task. They feel that no amount of effort made by them can alter the outcome. It is worth considering at this point that the rewards system operated in many schools perpetuates the idea of external motivation, that is, what motivates the child is a reward from another person rather than the pleasure to be found in discovering some new knowledge for its own sake. Encouraging a positive disposition in young children is fostered by giving choice, encouraging independence and offering interesting things for children to learn about, underpinned by loving support from a key person. Successful learning is an interweaving of confidence (emotion) and competence (cognition). As Jennie Lindon puts it, *'disposition is where thinking meets feeling'*.[5] The child who feels that she is truly a part of the group ('us') is likely to develop the emotional disposition to tackle new learning with all its uncertainties and possibilities for failure. She will be one of those children who demonstrate some of the characteristics of effective learning that are at the heart of the Early Years Foundation Stage curriculum. These characteristics, which are explored in Chapters 2, 3 and 4 of this book, are wholly dependent on a positive disposition to learning. Just as a reminder, they are:

1   Being involved and concentrating
2   Keeping on trying
3   Enjoying and achieving what they set out to do.

If we, as practitioners, can enable our children to develop these attitudes to learning we will have given them valuable skills, not just for their school journey but for their entire lives. All children will benefit from these positive habits of mind but those children who do not feel that they are 'us' will need more of our support to gain them.

Differences

Children who may not belong to the mainstream of our setting are almost impossible to classify. Some of our children will be on Action Plans and already have clearly defined needs to be addressed. However, what might be the needs of the quiet boy who does not enjoy playing superhero games or the child who finds gaining entrance into a role-play game impossible? We will consider just four types of difference in this chapter whilst recognising that, in reality, as the opening quote reminds us, children must all be treated fairly and all of them are unique and, thus, different.

Cultural difference

Settings vary enormously in the range of communities that they serve. I have worked in a nursery school that was situated in a community consisting of nearly all white families. I have also taught in areas that were rich in their cultural mix, the different groupings offering much to each other whilst at the same time needing support in terms of language and sometimes with gaining familiarity with routines and expectations. In retrospect, it was the setting in the one-dimensional community that was the most challenging in terms of deepening the children's knowledge of other cultures because our efforts felt rather like a nod in the direction of multiculturalism rather than offering a real insight into other communities, their customs, beliefs and values. I have heard this approach referred to as culture tourism and I feel we may have been guilty of that.

However, that said, as part of our efforts to raise our children's awareness of other communities we did invite a friend from the nearby city's Bangladeshi community to spend some time with us. As she arrived, one of our four-year-olds whispered to me '*Is she a princess?*' as she had come dressed in her glorious golden salwar kameez and lots of gold jewellery. She read stories in Urdu, cooked Chapattis and helped us paint beautiful patterns. I know that the day made a great impression on our children and the play and art and conversation that this time inspired was long-lasting. However, I am fully aware that this was not sufficient to develop a working knowledge and understanding of the multicultural world that my children would be joining. I was left with the feeling that my class of children were the ones who were, in a way, different because they had experienced such a small slice of how real life is lived and were not easily able to celebrate the differences all around them.

The school in the nearby city where I worked had a range of ethnicities within the catchment. It felt much more representational of life as it is now lived by the majority of the population. We marked a range of religious and cultural events, probably the most vibrant being the Eid parties that came at the end of a month-long period of fasting and restraint for the Muslim community. It was in this environment that a delicate interchange of information and expectations took place between the setting and its community, happily with the help of a support teacher with good language skills who could communicate meanings and intentions with sensitivity and understanding.

The cognitive development of children from communities that are different from the dominant one they will encounter in the early years setting is identical to the process of children who feel that they are in the majority. However, because of the difficulties arising from unfamiliarity with a whole range of everyday events such as routines, expectations, food and customs, cognitive development may look rather different or, indeed, be rather slower paced as children cope with the powerful need to feel at home, as their confidence builds before engaging with the struggle to, for example, read print in an additional language. Added to unfamiliarity is the fact that very young children lack the experience to understand exactly why there are such fundamental differences between their home and their setting and cannot articulate why they find expressing their intentions so hard. If there are racial tensions within the staff they must be tackled straight away, not least because of the requirements of the Race Relations Act of 2002 but also because these children are in particular need of feeling that they belong to this learning community. Interestingly, the New Zealand early years curriculum, which was devised to span two cultures, has as one of its major strands, 'belonging'. It poses a question from a young child in response to each of its five strands and the question for belonging is '*Is this place fair for us?*'

'*Fairness*' is a straightforward way to describe exactly what the young child from a minority group needs to experience to thrive intellectually. Staffs need to question the fairness of, for example, expecting young Muslim children, particularly girls, to undress to go into the paddling pool or showing impatience with children who are used to using different implements for eating. The emotional damage that continued insensitivity may cause is very likely to damage these children's emerging self-confidence and impede their progress towards developing a positive disposition to learning. Thus, not feeling at home has a direct impact on their ability to thrive cognitively.

Children with a cultural difference may well have difficulties in showing adults in the setting what they do understand and have learned. Practitioners must not make assumptions about children's levels of development but must use observation and family or liaison teacher knowledge to discover as accurately as possible where the child is with learning and development. For example, a bucket of water and a paintbrush in the outside area will enable a Chinese child to paint his name in Mandarin script on the ground when he might not have felt confident enough to use pencil and paper indoors. When his efforts are praised, progress is likely to follow. Young children are well aware of their differences and are sensitive to them. It is the practitioners who must reassure children that their differences are both acceptable and positive and that they are in a setting which genuinely celebrates difference and diversity.

Gender difference

At the end of the twentieth century, research into gender difference was not encouraged. It was felt that for young children to be offered equal opportunities to learn, they should be treated equally, and that this meant, the same. This is now recognised as being counterproductive as equality of opportunity is clearly not helped by forcing a large group of unique and disparate individuals to all learn in the same ways.

You do not have to be a trained early years practitioner to recognise the startling differences between boys and girls. My own education in this aspect of gender difference came as a grandmother when regularly spending time with my grandson. His preferences were in stark contrast to those of my two daughters and his older sister. I have lost count of the hours we have stood watching workmen digging holes in the ground. Even if it was pouring with rain he would refuse to move away and became knowledgeable at a very young age about the different names of heavy moving equipment. On one occasion I remember a particularly friendly workman suggesting that we join his gang as we seemed to spend so much time there. After a typical trail round south London's building sites we would reach home to spend a little time relaxing with a book. Out would come the all-time favourite, *Dig, Dig, Digger*[6], and careful attention would be given to the names and attributes of the various pieces of equipment. I would be gently reprimanded by this three-year-old as I mistook one type of lorry for another. '*No, Granny, that's not a trailer, it's a low loader*' was typical of the exchanges we would have as he tried to increase my knowledge to match his.

Figure 7.1 *Understanding what it is to be male*

It has been interesting for me watching this little boy's progress through his early years setting. He is gentle by nature and finds superhero play difficult as he often finds himself cast as a 'baddie' through a combination of a lack of TV acumen and having a generally affable personality. This situation has led to him needing some support from his early years team as he has had to negotiate his way to a social position in the group that he feels comfortable with. His key person has responded with insightful professionalism, spending time in the outside play area with the 'superheros' and finding that difficult balance between valuing rough and tumble play and supporting those boys who find it challenging.

My grandson's literacy development had differed significantly from his sister's too. He had the same home encouragement and the same early years experiences in learning to read but found a completely different way into reading. As is common with boys, he found the structure of phonics helpful and greatly enjoyed the playful way his school introduced it.

In allowing both genders the freedom to learn in a way that suits them, it seems to me that very good work has been started with helping young girls to feel that life's opportunities are opening up. I worry very much about the culture of the 'pink princess' which links dangerously into the celebrity culture and thus limits girls' visions of what might be achievable for them. However, I feel that there is even more work to be done in the field of helping boys towards understanding what it is to be male, especially in those families where there is no constant male figure and the media image of the stereotypical male is excessively physical and non-verbal. Both these extremes are inherently damaging to children's cognition as they affect children's ability to think creatively and narrow their aspirations to society's current norms. Practitioners have a huge responsibility to remember, and to act on the adage, that education, if it is about anything, is about opening up opportunities and not closing them down.

Ability difference

Thinking about disability, and even the terminology used to describe disability, is always changing as attitudes change, medical progress is made and the views of people with disabilities change. An example of this is in the stroke unit of our local hospital where the nursing and specialist team never refer to someone who has had a stroke as a 'stroke victim' but as 'someone who has had a stroke'. This use of language, refusing as it does to label someone as a 'victim', is considered to be empowering, sensitive and, above all, accurate. The professional view is that as soon as someone sees themselves as a victim, their prognosis can diminish due to the perceived helplessness of their situation. This perception of the expected outcome of their medical condition will affect how a patient views their prospects, lessening the likelihood of progress towards recovery. It is in this way that mind and body can be seen to interact and cognitive processes thus affect the course of recovery.

In much the same way, children who have particular educational needs can sometimes believe themselves to be unable to alter their situation in any way because of their victim-like status. They become receivers of special care, which they undoubtedly need, but do not think that they themselves have anything to offer to their community; that they can give as well as receive. Recently, social attitudes have begun to alter as, for example, actors with disabilities are performing on stage and prime-time TV. The Paralympics, for example, give an opportunity for those with learning and behavioural needs to shine and to feel the same sense of achievement and wellbeing as all other sportspeople and their delight in their successes is joyous to see.

Even more radical, perhaps, is that the medical model of disability is rapidly giving way to what is known as the social model whereby certain groups of people with disabilities, in particular the deaf community, do not see themselves as deficient. What they perceive is that the society in which they live is not well adapted to their needs. It is not they who need to change, but society which needs to adapt so that deaf people can have fulfilling lives which are equal in all opportunities.

These ideas, which are gaining ground in our communities, are reflected in our early years settings, and with good reason. All that we now know about how people view themselves, with the resulting levels of confidence, wellbeing and high self-esteem, tells us those children who are different need to be given high, yet realistic expectations, just like all children. They need to be helped to know what is possible for them and to be encouraged to push their individual boundaries. Perhaps a useful attitude is integration rather than inclusion. Integration suggests a gathering of a wide range of individuals, all valued and respected, rather than a less appropriate effort to meld a variety of children into a one-size-fits-all set of expectations.

Wealth difference

No discussion on difference written at this time of economic hardship would be complete without a consideration of the effects of poverty on children's intellectual development. 'Poverty Goes Straight to the Brain'[7] is one of a number of similar articles reflecting ongoing research, mainly from the USA, which suggests direct links between some parts of brain function and childhood poverty. The argument broadly suggests that the seven indicators of poverty, encompassing standard elements such as maternal mental illness, lack of employment, low income and overcrowded living conditions, lead to raised stress levels. This chronic and cumulative stress leads to raised levels of cortisol in the brain which would appear to affect, in particular, memory and language function. An effective working memory is essential for the development of creativity and critical thinking skills which are necessary tools for a successful adult life.

In order to provide effectively for children coping with these difficulties it behoves practitioners to be aware of the fundamental disadvantages that poverty causes and to ensure that their settings are places of calm and consistency and they provide nutritious and regular food. This physical and emotionally nurturing environment will not only help to balance children's highly charged feelings but is a first step towards feeding their brains too.

In conclusion it is clear that there are many types of difference, all of which need different responses. It is helpful to remember that all development follows a broadly similar pattern and that children who have particular needs will not require a 'special needs solution' but will move forwards in somewhat different ways or at a rather different pace. What is a universal fact is that all children, however different, need to be respected and nurtured and to feel that they are part of 'us' to develop their full intellectual potential.

Challenges and dilemmas

- Practitioners need to question philosophies which are dominant and ask whether they are, in fact, those best suited to children's learning. A 'one-size-fits-all' remedy to a perceived deficit, such as reading, may induce feelings of failure and then be counter productive.
- Support all children to feel that they are part of 'us' when they are in the setting. Plan to support difference and minority in the less expected areas such as gender and poverty.

CHAPTER 8

Thoughtful organisation

Early years teams using identical buildings can, and do, create totally different settings for children's learning.[1]

This opening quotation leads into a chapter that is concerned both with the ethos and the practicalities of leading practice. These two strands are inseparable and it is proposed to take each in turn to explore how they impact on each other. There will be a consideration as to how organisation can either facilitate or impede children's cognitive development and how some of the characteristics of effective learning can be supported or limited by the organisation of provision and the management of daily routines.

Ethos

Before any decision is made about how to organise an early years setting the team need to know what they are trying to achieve. In Chapter 1, a debate about differing philosophies of education considered the current view of learning theory known as social constructivism. This has a view of the young child as potentially strong, autonomous and capable. To unlock this potential and turn it into a reality, each young child needs to be loved and will, because of this, develop a high sense of self-esteem. It is self-esteem that gives the child courage to explore what new concepts there are to be understood and try out new skills that they will need to become competent. These are some of the underlying principles of social constructivism:

- children are potentially strong and autonomous learners
- children need loving and sensitive adults to be their companions
- children's view of themselves is key to their success as learners
- play is a powerful mechanism that enables children to develop their understandings
- what children can do should be the starting point of their future learning.

As stated in Chapter 1, central to this understanding is the view that learning is an active mental and individual effort to construct meaning. This belief does not sit well with what is often called the 'skills and drills' approach seen in many primary schools with its emphasis on passive rote learning in large group sessions and measurable targets.

The setting that holds to the principles of social constructivism will base their organisation and daily routines on them. This will lead to the organising of the setting to provide for children to be:

- active
- playful
- independent
- reflective
- collaborative
- exploratory
- creative
- critical thinkers.

These ways of learning will encourage children's cognitive development and subsequently instil in them positive dispositions to learning. When these dispositions are in place children will be seen displaying the attributes of effective learners such as persistence, problem-solving and critical and creative thinking.

Children who are being helped to learn in this way will also be acquiring the cognitive attributes that they need to learn effectively. Their working memory will be nourished and they will be learning new concepts through schematic and imaginative play. Role play will also help them develop Theory of Mind which will lessen their egocentricity and introduce them to the life-long tools needed to conduct successful co-operation and friendships. Those very young children who feel emotionally secure in the presence of their key person will be more able to deal with the cognitive and emotional challenge of the comings and goings of their primary carer, a regular experience which requires flexible and sensitive handling when routines are being devised.

In practical terms, the setting has to be a place that is, first, emotionally secure so that every child can feel that they belong.

Second, it must be a place full of interesting things to do and to find out about and a place where practising developing concepts and skills is valued as part of the process of consolidating what is partly known and becomes understanding that is securely embedded and can be used as the basis for the next step of learning.

The practicalities

From the principles stated above and the associated list of attributes associated with them it is possible to deduce how a setting can be arranged in order to help young children learn most effectively. It was the government report of 1990, the so-called 'Rumbold' report[2] that clearly stated that, in the early years, how children were taught was every bit as important as what they were taught. As more recent

Figure 8.1 *Self managing learners*

neurological research has enabled us to see how young children's brains respond to their surroundings it would seem probable that it is in fact more important to concentrate on how children are taught and not to get too concerned with the curriculum content.

We know from research that, for example, children under the age of six are self-managing learners. This means that their motivation to learn what they are curious about is much stronger than their ability to learn what others wish them to learn. This has implications for how the setting needs to be organised in terms of the balance between adult-initiated and child-initiated learning. This particular point was illustrated by the story of Daisy and London's water-recycling system described in Chapter 3. Children need to be able to learn playfully in an environment that is loving, reciprocal and stress-free. They need to be able to explore, to watch others, to interact and to build on what they already know. As Julie Fisher suggests in *Starting from the Child*, children need to have their learning structured so that they can learn '*actively, interactively and independently*'.[3]

The type of organisation that will put in place the elements to provide a challenging yet secure learning environment relies entirely on the staff understanding and implementing, with confidence, the systems that are in place. This is more likely to happen if the team is well trained and believe in what they are doing. The lead practitioner will need to explain, negotiate and be clear and firm about the principles that make up the setting's ethos whilst retaining flexibility and a responsive approach when there is resistance and misunderstanding. It is probably the most daunting aspect of leading practice but, none the less, the most rewarding when the whole adult team can see the results of a calm and confidently run setting on the children who will, themselves, become calm and confident and display the characteristics of effective learning. Below are some of the basic practicalities that need to be considered.

Daily routines

The pattern of the day is central to how confident children, and adults, feel about their setting and their place within it. It helps children's confidence and independence if, for example, they know that when they arrive, they can find something straight away that they want to do. It may be some new activity that they have found really intriguing or it may be an activity that they know they are competent at and want to share with their carer. Adults may need to have a quick word with a member of staff about the child or an aspect of family life. Staff must, therefore, be available for this and organise the start of the day to accommodate the needs of both children and their parents.

Settings who begin the day with a whole-group registration process will find the early arrivals restless by the time the late arrivals have settled in, and the adults who need a little attention will either not be afforded any or will make the start of the group session even more delayed. Looked at through the eyes of the young child, motivation is centred on immediately completing yesterday's model, talking to a new friend or reading a favourite book and not sitting on the carpet inactively, waiting for a tedious registration session. How the child begins each session significantly affects both the emotional and cognitive processes. Learning and the motivation to learn are enabled by the child's ability to immediately get involved in what interests them. The organisation of routines is not for the benefit of adult management but to enhance children's motivation to learn. Many settings have thought through the start of their sessions and come up with imaginative alternative ways of registering which children are present. Settings that have devised systems of self-registration and provided activities for children to get started on as soon as they arrive will find that this also frees up a few moments to greet parents. A slightly staggered arrival time then is also possible, allowing for variations in families' early morning patterns as well as a less rushed feel to this, most crucial, part of the session, where time needs to be taken to help this transition time to be calm and less stressful for adults and children.

Despite all we now know about the benefits to the cognitive development of children of being active, interactive and independent, research carried out in 2010 by Janet Moyles and Maulfrey Worthington found that, particularly in reception classes, *'children spent over a third of their day in being occupied in whole class sessions'*.[4] Routines such as snack times, outside play times and group review times must take into account that, particularly for these very young children, it is developmentally inappropriate for them to spend very much time as part of a large group. Cognitively, many very young children will appear inattentive in these sessions because they do not appreciate that an adult addressing a large group of children is also talking to them individually. The young child's home experience of talk is of individually targeted conversations, normally as a result of a child's question. In other words, at home children get to ask the questions but, at nursery, they usually find themselves trying to find answers to other people's questions about which they are not always very interested.

Other routines that will support children's active and independent learning are those that allow children to move around between activities and areas of provision at will. They will decide when they have finished playing with, for example, the water and will gain nothing from being made to stay longer once the motivation has ended. Persistence and concentration are attributes that need to be fostered but will occur naturally and more powerfully if the activity or provision is interesting enough. Often, children's observed movement from place to place can be linked to how engaging the provision is and sometimes it is due to the developmental level of, say, the new child who is genuinely excited by all they see and have not been attending long enough to appreciate that it will all still be available the next time they come. That gives a strong message to the setting about the nature of provision. It must be constant to provide consistency and yet flexible to allow for challenge and interest to be maintained.

Resources

These are the tools that practitioners have to help them implement the curriculum. The most valuable resource that a setting has is its adult staff. Perhaps the commitments of the Early Years Foundation Stage could be thought of as applying to the adults in the setting as well as the children? Each adult is unique and has individual strengths and areas for development. If the setting is to be an enabling environment for the adults working there, each adult must feel that their personal and professional development is valued and encouraged. To ensure positive relationships amongst the adult team, the lead practitioner will need to know each member of staff well, and be entirely professional in dealing with all adults equally, helping them each to feel that they belong to the workplace in just the same way that the children do. The commitment of learning and development is about the growth and sustainability of the setting, what it aims to achieve and the part that each individual plays in its evaluation and development plan.

With the adult team feeling nurtured and confident, the setting is well placed to make full use of its other resources. These are often thought of as being time, space and equipment. An understanding of the ethos of the setting leads directly to the ways in which these are organised. For children to be active and creative, there needs to be a careful balance of things to do that are planned for by the practitioners and those that are in the control of the child. The former are often referred to as activities and the latter as provision. Children must be helped to understand how the resources are to be used, for example, whether the dolls may be taken to the outside den or the bricks used in the sand. Research shows that the more freedom children have in their use of materials and the more choices they can make as to what purpose to put their chosen resources, the more complex will be the play and, consequently, the higher will be the cognitive levels of learning.[5] This is usually discernible by the increased level of complex exchanges of spoken language observed in the course of the play. We are reminded of this in card 4.3 which states '*children will more easily make connections between things if the environment encourages them to do so. For example, they need to be able to fetch materials easily and to be able to move them from one place to another.*'

Material resources require several levels of thoughtfulness if they are to succeed in raising cognitive levels in children. Firstly, they need to be fit for purpose, in other words, well-ordered and attractive to use. At a very basic level, they do not need to be necessarily the most expensive but they must be clean, organised so that children can access them without adult help and regularly maintained so that pencils are sharp, painting water clean and puzzles all complete. Creativity and critical thinking is not likely to emerge if children are expected to use shabby equipment.

The second level of thoughtfulness concerns the breadth of learning opportunities contained within each resource. This means that some consideration must be given as to whether the resource is capable of stretching the thought processes of the able child as well as providing those more straightforward experiences that a new learner needs. How resources are set up and offered for use will determine how broadly they appeal. An example of this is the role-play area where a challenging cafe with its menu writing and calculating of bills will not necessarily appeal to the youngest children who always need their basic home play facilities. Provision for progression in learning is one of the major advantages that play has as children can independently choose the appropriate level of learning for them.

Similarly, creativity will be stifled if another major resource is poorly used, that of time. For anyone, child or adult, to get deeply immersed in a creation, be that physical, artistic, literary or scientific, the prime requirement is time; and lots of it. Time needs to be available in long sessions, not truncated by snack times and other interventions that might satisfy perceived managerial requirements but will lessen children's ability to develop intellectual skills such as persistence and concentration. Children will also need time to become familiar with materials before they can engage at a high cognitive level with them. EYFS card 4.1 suggests, '*Children who are allowed to play with resources and equipment before using them to solve a problem are more likely to solve the problem successfully.*' Everyday opportunities to become familiar with materials will result in high levels of satisfaction and competence.

Flexible use of time and space also allows for children's brains to make new connections as their understandings are transformed and clarified. Unusual or different combinations of materials such as, for example, a large ball of ice in the water tray, instead of the normal bubbles, will spark curiosity and promote questions such as '*How did that happen?*' or '*Can we make it water again?*' This type of thinking is known as divergent and it challenges children to wonder '*What else is possible?*' Divergent thinking is not limited to what are thought of as the creative arts but applies to every aspect of life where there is more than one possible answer. On an everyday level it possible to encourage children to think in a divergent way about, perhaps, how the domestic role-play area could be differently arranged to suit children's current play themes or what equipment could be included in an off-the-ground trail around the outside area. It is for this reason that convergent thought is generally to be discouraged in the setting as a culture that emphasises only right and wrong answers and is not one that will encourage children to brainstorm ideas, have a go, or experiment just for the joy of seeing what happens.

Space is a resource that is sometimes poorly understood and very often settings will struggle with constraints as to the amount of the space they have been allocated. Generally speaking, children need a lot of space to play actively without being trampled on by others and quarrels will often erupt if there is insufficient room for children to follow their ideas through, giving play a bad name. Adults need to be sensitive to this, placing activities that need a lot of room as far away as possible from areas such as the book corner where children have come to enjoy a story and will not appreciate excited shouting or dripping paint. Often, the thoughtful management of these very practical aspects such as the placing and staffing of activities makes all the difference between a successful learning experience and a frustrating and negative one. The positioning of furniture into bays or contained areas will have a huge impact on how children use the resources within these areas. The very fact of the enclosure will slow children's speed, help them to commit to an activity or area of provision and keep them there longer which enables a deeper investigation at a calmer pace. This is a non-verbal and non-confrontational strategy and its effects are somewhat similar to what is often referred to as the hidden curriculum in that it is not overt but nonetheless influential and successful in achieving its aims. The aim in this case is to give opportunities for thoughtful reflection, divergent thinking and considered questioning.

Play

Play, and the adult's role in it, is known to be crucial to successfully growing the characteristics of effective learning. The following are some of the attributes of play which have a beneficial effect on cognitive growth:

- It is enjoyable. We know from our own experiences of learning something new, that it is more successful if it is made an enjoyable process.
- It enables children to learn in ways in which they are hard-wired to learn: actively, interactively and independently. If we teach children in ways that link with how they naturally develop, their learning will make sense to them and it is more likely to be securely understood and remembered.
- Play helps children to enter alternative worlds. Through play children can drive trains, make cups of tea, feed the baby and put themselves in the place of others. They can experience what it might be like to be someone else or feeling as someone else does. The development of cognitive attributes such as symbolic representation, empathy and Theory of Mind are practised and refined in children's role play.

- Play can be organised to cater for a range of learners' needs. It can be straight-forward, such as domestic role play, or it can be complex such as a shipwreck game, thereby catering for children at different levels of cognitive development. It also helps children to learn in other ways than the purely academic, although a high level of thinking is often involved in imaginative play. Many children learn through physical expression rather than through maths or literacy; there are children who shine musically or creatively. Rich playful learning encompasses the learning styles of all these children, acknowledging that each child is unique and needs to be provided with learning opportunities that enable them individually to succeed.

- Play can offer children control over their learning. In so many other aspects of young children's lives they cannot exercise any control. It is well understood that adults who feel the happiest are those who feel that they can make decisions that are respected and can direct and organise substantial aspects of their lives. Children cannot decide much about what happens to them on a daily basis but if they can be offered choices during their time in the setting they will gain attributes which significantly help their social, emotional and cognitive development. If children are encouraged to take responsibility in their play, choose their resources, their time scale, their friends and their goals, they will learn how to exercise control responsibly, learning empathy for others and feeling the wellbeing and satisfaction that accompanies the completion and ownership of a challenging piece of learning. The treasure basket is a valuable resource in providing babies with the opportunity to choose and take control of a new resource in much the same way as older children make choices in their play.

- Possibly the most useful aspect of play from the educational point of view is its ability to act as an integrating mechanism. Rich play experiences allow for children to bring together, or integrate everything that they know, feel and can do to a new piece of learning. A helpful example of this might be the child who decides to paint a picture of an owl having read the story *The Owl Babies*. There needs to be an integration of what the child knows about owls (fluffy, grey, big wings, flies at night) with what they can do (mix black and white paint, draw an owl shape, perhaps stick on feathers). These developmental aspects need to be integrated into what the child feels (a desire or motivation to create an owl and a belief that it is possible). These three areas need to be used in conjunction with each other to enable a successful outcome. Of course, both the availability of suitable resources and the adult's role in this process is paramount.

The adult's role

As stated above, to play a full role in children's learning the adult team need to feel nurtured and confident. Each member of the team must understand the development of young children, the ways in which they learn and how to interpret the curriculum for children in developmentally appropriate ways.

These are some of the practical ways in which an adult can usefully support young children as they seek new understandings:

- Plan for children's experiences based on observation and assessment to identify children's interests and abilities.
- Build loving relationships with their key children so that they are able to take risks, accept, overcome and use minor failures.
- Stimulate and sustain children's interest.
- Extend and challenge children's thinking.
- Inform and instruct on use of equipment.
- Model behaviour which is likely to encourage experimentation, divergent thinking and creativity.
- Communicate with other adults involved in children's learning such as other team members and parents.

It is while the adults are supporting children's learning in the ways outlined above that they are able to engage in one of the most valuable strategies for developing cognitive processes, the one that we continually return to of *sustained shared thinking*.[6] The REPEY report into the quality of young children's settings found that this type of open-ended interaction was key to promoting higher-level thinking skills in young children. It defines sustained shared thinking as:

> an episode in which two or more individuals 'work together' in an intellectual way to solve a problem, clarify a concept, evaluate activities, extend a narrative etc. Both parties must contribute to the thinking and it must develop and extend.

It becomes clear that the adult who is truly able to help children develop their cognitive abilities needs a wide range of skills. It is whilst observing, modelling, informing, extending, communicating about and loving the children for whom they have responsibility that their key children will flourish in the nurturing environment that has been put in place around them.

Challenges and dilemmas

- Beware of routines that have been in place for a very long time and have not been recently reassessed and justified. Children's time in settings is limited and must not be wasted in activities that benefit adult organisation rather than children's learning.
- All routines need to be based on a sound philosophy. Establish the vision first and the practicalities will follow from it. Do not be tempted to fit a belief into a routine; it has to be the other way round.

CHAPTER 9

Equipped for life, ready for school?

A school is a community in which children learn to live first and foremost as children and not as future adults.[1]

The title of this chapter is taken from Dame Tickell's independent report on the Early Years Foundation Stage, now mandatory. It makes the assumption that being equipped for life and being ready for school is one and the same thing. This chapter will question that assumption and look in depth at how the characteristics of effective learning, that are at the heart of this book, can help children access what is on offer at key stage one.

It is clear from the messages coming from government that its priority is to ensure that young children entering key stage one have the necessary skills to take advantage of the largely formal, transmission model of teaching that predominates in many year one and the majority of year two classrooms. In response to the Tickell report, Sarah Teather, Children's minister, said this:

> I am pleased that Clare [Tickell] has focused on what really matters – making sure a child is able to start school ready to learn, able to make friends and play, ready to ask for what they need and say what they think. These are critical foundations for really getting the best out of school.

It is perhaps helpful to begin by analysing the kind of learning environment that a child entering key stage one is likely to find. Julie Fisher, in her book *Moving on to Key Stage One*, comments:

> In 2004, Ofsted produced a report entitled *Transition from the Reception Year to Year 1*. Its findings suggested that insufficient consideration was being given to the relationship between the curricula in the Foundation Stage and in Year 1 and that transition to more formal approaches in Year 1 was sometimes too 'abrupt'. In particular, inspectors highlighted that in some schools, emphasis was given to the two national strategies at the expense of regular attention to other subjects.[2]

Similarly, Guy Claxton referred to these formal approaches in his 2012 Graham Nuttall annual lecture entitled '*Can Schools Prepare You for Anything*?' He suggests a list of attitudes and activities that primary schools across the world are asking of their pupils on a daily basis:

- being right
- listening to the teacher
- working alone
- following instructions
- copying down
- accepting what you are told
- sitting still
- showing respect
- being evaluated.

He asks what could be the result of training children to think and behave in these ways on a regular basis. One might suggest, perhaps, compliance, passivity, isolation and low self-esteem. Professor Claxton suggested, somewhat wryly, that these habits of mind would be more suitable for a nineteenth-century clerk than a twenty-first-century explorer.[3]

There would appear then, to be at the very least, a gulf between the pedagogy of the Foundation Stage and that of mainstream schooling but, sadly, the picture is worse than that. In their recent research for TACTYC (the Association for the Professional Development of Early Years Educators), Janet Moyles and Maulfrey Worthington looked at the daily experiences of children currently in the reception year of the Foundation Stage in England. They found that the ambitions of the EYFS were '*largely unrealised*'.[4] One of the major tenets of the EYFS, for example, was the assertion that '*In their play, children learn at their highest level.*'[5] Yet, Moyles and Worthington found '*little provision for rich and unpredictable play and learning*'. This finding describes a position similar to that of earlier research undertaken in 2004 by the Association of Teachers and Lecturers.

The observers in that research saw few opportunities for:
- sustained, shared and purposeful talk
- sustained, complex and imaginative play
- authentic, engaging, first-hand experiences.[6]

Given that these three aspects of early years education and care form the kernel of the EYFS and, indeed, of the independent report by Clare Tickell, who talks consistently of '*active exploring, creativity and critical thinking*',[7] it would seem appropriate to attempt to unravel some of the muddled thinking that appears to be clouding the vision of many EYFS practitioners. Practitioners talk consistently to researchers of their belief in and passion for play but, in reality, are able to provide little in the way of enabling environments for rich and unpredictable first-hand play experiences.

Curricula and pedagogy

One of the most muddled pieces of thinking is evident in the title of this chapter. The assumption that being equipped for life and being ready for school are one and the same thing is false. In fact, being ready for school implies being prepared for a fixed standard of physical, intellectual and social demands. Young children need to be trained to cope with aspects of a school's cognitive curriculum, such as linguistic and mathematical skills, which are most straight-forwardly delivered and measured in whole class, solitary and silent formats. Guy Claxton's list from the Graham Nuttall annual lecture, quoted above, provides evidence of the reality of the teaching styles and expectations adopted by the majority of schools.

Being ready for life, however, is much more concerned with the character-istics of effective learning on which this book is centred. One of the fundamental attributes of being ready for life is that of self-regulation. This is based on the notion that children who have both motivation and ability, sometimes called the 'skill and the will', are those most ready to succeed in life and take advantage of all it has to offer. Self-regulation is sometimes thought of as a positive disposition, incorporating self-belief and strategies necessary to think laterally. It combines aspects of both cognitive and emotional development as high estimations of what children feel, both about themselves and about their abilities, are necessary to attain the competence and control of the successful learner.

Self-regulation involves being able to regulate feelings and behaviour as appro-priate and to delay gratification and to communicate ideas and express views. Some elements are key to the development of self-regulation. They include:

- autonomy
- high self-belief
- good communication skills
- a rich environment
- loving adult companions.

All these elements are happily to be found in a setting where child-initiated and unpredictable play is cherished. The Foundation Stage curriculum emphasised that '*Play and other imaginative and creative activities help children to make sense of their experience and "transform" their knowledge, fostering cognitive development.*'[8] Here the Department for Education and Schools is suggesting that a significant part of preparing children for life is to support their cognitive development and that play is the most effective tool that we have to achieve that aim. It would appear that government documentation is clear in its support for environments that support the development of learners for life, but the reality is different. We therefore find ourselves with a pedagogy, or belief system, that supports equipping children for life but a curriculum, as it often interpreted, concerned with getting children ready for school.

Figure 9.1 *Play fosters creative and cognitive development*

Realities and practicalities

The stresses of attempting to tie together being equipped for life with readiness for school are apparent in the Tickell report. Tickell suggests that children's unreadiness for school includes children being '*not yet toilet trained, unable to listen or to get on with other children*'.[9]

Toilet training

Most children are toilet trained by the time they enter reception class. Many still need some help, which is quite appropriate, particularly for those children who may enter a reception class a full year younger than their peers. Any exasperation on the part of teachers will only exacerbate a sensitive situation rather than resolving it and it is perhaps an indication that a formal school environment is not the most appropriate one in which to place small children for long periods of time.

A major part of this first stage of education is helping children in the progression of social skills and one of these is personal care. Practitioners must acknowledge that time will need to be spent on helping children acquire self-care skills such as toileting alongside others such as dressing, washing and feeding. At this stage of their lives these self-help skills are every bit as important as reading and writing and, it could be argued, in terms of creating confident and independent young people, probably more important. Those children who are self-organising and autonomous are more likely to be those who will have the self-confidence to think 'Yes, I can do that', when it comes to tackling the high-level literary skills that will be demanded of them at key stage one.

Listening

Very young children are perfectly able to listen, having been listening to their mother's voice since before birth. A child soon after birth demonstrates the motivation and ability to listen attentively and respond to the voice of their parent or carer. This type of communication is always on a one-to-one basis and is sometimes referred to as a 'dance'; that is, a two-way interaction where each partner has an important part. What is meant by listening in the context of the primary school is a very different affair. The young child will be sitting with many others, probably attending, rather than listening, to ideas that are in the teacher's head rather than in the child's head. Often what has to be listened to seems meaningless to them and, developmentally, the young child does not always understand that a teacher addressing a large group is also talking to them individually. This type of activity is, for these developmental reasons, often doomed to failure but what needs to be remedied is the purpose and design of the conversation, not the child.

Often, the purpose of whole-group times on the carpet seems to centre on adult-focused activities such as registration or the tedious weather chart. The child can see no purpose in either of these daily events and, as we know, a child's main driving aim is to make sense out of what they are experiencing. If no sense can be made of what is happening, a child will look around for something else that catches their interest instead. This may be the Velcro fastening of the shoes of the child sitting nearby or the long hair of the child in front. These daily chores have very little to do with preparing children for life and much more to do with crowd control.

Getting on with other children

The Tickell report is also concerned about children's abilities to get on with other children. For social skills to be developed children need to spend long periods of time playing, negotiating, taking turns, being respected, being autonomous and being listened to. These experiences are just the sort that a good preschool setting will provide. Social skills will not develop easily if the practice is informed by the prescribed curriculum with its emphasis on whole-group literacy sessions, passivity and conformity. What is needed for the development of both social and cognitive skills is, as the Association of Teachers and Lecturers (ATL) research in 2004 found, 'sustained, shared and purposeful talk, complex and imaginative play and authentic and engaging experiences'.[10]

Very often the phrase 'share nicely' is heard in early years settings. Practitioners with a sound knowledge of child development will understand how inappropriate a command this is as the very young child, with a yet underdeveloped sense of empathy, will often need to claim possession of a required resource as a demonstration of their developing identity. This situation is best dealt with by gentle explanation and, crucially, generous resourcing in terms of equipment, time and space. Young children can, and do, demonstrate great care and understanding of each other's needs and will, when at the appropriate stage of development, play co-operatively and engage in deep friendships. What will encourage these particular behaviours and habits of mind are responsive and sensitive practitioners and thoughtfully planned resourcing which encourage children to play together in an unstressed and stimulating environment.

Literacy

Lastly, the Tickell report states, '*We do children no favours if we fail to prepare them for the realities of the school environment where skills such as literacy are at a premium.*' Literacy, in its broadest sense, is at a premium long before children enter formal schooling. Babies communicate with their families from the moment of birth and are consummately successful at getting their needs met from that point onwards. Spoken language is acquired with increasing speed and sophistication throughout the toddler years and if there is an emphasis on real reasons to talk, reason and negotiate in the Foundation Stage, these literacy skills will develop apace. Stories, rhymes and songs will increase children's delight in literacy, preparing them in the best possible way for learning to read and write when that time comes.

The tone of the quotation from the Tickell report above, however, seems to suggest that to prepare children effectively for '*the realities*' of literacy at key stage one, children need to be subjected to formal sessions of invented systems such as synthetic phonics and the rote learning of sounds and words. The probable end result of following this course of action is that children will be neither well equipped for life or ready for school as their confidence will evaporate in the face of inappropriately styled learning activities.

Three types of readiness

An occasional paper from TACTYC suggested that children's readiness might be thought of in several different ways.[11]

1 Readiness for learning.
2 Readiness for school
3 The readiness of the school for the child.

Readiness for learning

As the above paper reminds us, '*children's learning is limited only by their lack of experience and accumulated knowledge*' and not by any deficit in intelligence. All the tools that children need to both grow and become aware of their emotional, physical, social and cognitive skills are in place and developing fast from birth onwards. The view of children as strong and eager learners is one that fits well within the paradigm of social constructivism where young learners fit together their own new understandings from their personal experiences. Worryingly, however, current government anxieties about falling measurements of older children's academic and social gains have placed a skewed emphasis on goals that the child entering the reception class has yet to achieve such as reliable toileting, reading, writing and sharing possessions. These are seen as faults to be corrected by formal systems and strategies which can instil in a child feelings of anxiety and failure if they do not understand what is required of them and with which they are not developmentally able to comply.

As the government report, 'Starting with Quality' (otherwise known as the Rumbold report) stated in 1990, *'For the early years educator, the process of education – how children are encouraged to learn – is as important as, and inseparable from, the content – what they learn.'*[12] What we know both from neuroscience and from contemporary child development theory is that the most successful new learning is founded on aspects of children's experiences that are meaningful to them and that they understand more deeply when learning is about processes rather than about correct answers. The 'how' of teaching young children can thus be seen as a mix of activities that offer a large amount of success, a motivating amount of interest, a flexible end-point, an appropriate amount of challenge and a responsive adult taking one of a number of possible roles. The following example provides an illustration of such a piece of learning.

Staff in a 39-place nursery school in a rural location had followed the interest shown by a group of children about homes. The interest had arisen from the cage that had been provided for the resident hamster and there was much discussion about how different homes suited different occupants and how they would not like to live in a cage. During the next few days staff placed a shoe box in the nursery with a label alongside which said '*Who lives here?*' A clue was offered in the form of painted footprints going into and around the house, which the children variously identified as a mouse, a dinosaur and a wolf! This was just enough to motivate curiosity amongst some of the older children who constructed a small house from cardboard and placed a different small-world creature inside each day. They made a range of small footprints and asked the adults to guess the current occupant, delighting in each wrong answer.

There was no end-product in this piece of learning but it provided oppor- tunities for deep levels of thinking, analysis, research, reflection and progression of understanding amongst the children. All these processes are helpful in the formation of habits of mind which are an intrinsic part of developing successful life-long learning. There were also opportunities for children to explore processes connected with construction, print making, making labels and imaginative play as they thought of other clues, such as feathers, to help identify the inhabitants of the box. There was evidence of deep satisfaction in children's accomplishments as they made up the stories that accompanied the house ownership and this progressed to redesigning the role-play area to become the wolf's house, complete with disguises, granny's bonnet, mirrors and a small red cape. The enthusiasm which accompanied this piece of learning was evidence of how very young children can successfully learn in this less formal and playful way and the observations made by the adults confirmed their view that children were operating cognitively, socially and emotionally at a high level. This type of learning was also observed to offer the children opportunities to acquire the characteristics of effective learning that have been explored in this book, specifically, being involved and concentrating, enjoying what they set out to do and choosing new ways to do things.

Readiness for school

Contrary to the received wisdom that ensuring readiness for school involves starting formal learning ever earlier, those with an understanding of child development will know that the children who are best prepared for school are those who have received the experiences they need at the appropriate level for their current stage of development. Those children who have been able to explore playfully and experience success at ages three and four and who have gained a positive self-image will be those who will cope most confidently with the more formal tasks that come their way at key stage one. This is not to suggest that formal learning is appropriate at key stage one, for children at age six are not significantly different in their learning styles and needs than those at age five. However, children who have a high self-esteem, and have experienced learning that has been presented in ways similar to the scenario described above, will enter the next stage of their education with a positive disposition to learning, confident and competent.

The quote at the head of this chapter from the Plowden report is just as relevant today as when it was written, asserting that the children who are best prepared for school are those who have received what they need as children. They are, first and foremost, children of today and not adults of tomorrow.

The readiness of school for the child

Readiness is sometimes defined as the match between the readiness of the child and the readiness of the environments that serve young children. If one of the goals of early years education is to provide an environment where children are helped to become aware of and responsible for their own cognitive development (self-regulation), there are clear indicators that will further this ambition. At this point, it might be sensible to emphasise the word 'if' because, as David Whitebread reminds us in his recent work on school readiness, *'The disagreement about terminology and definition belies a fundamental difference in conception of the purpose of early years education.'*[13] For as long as the purpose of early years education is mired in confusion, so then will be the ensuing pedagogy and the practice, both of which need to be based on a secure foundation of agreed purpose.

These are big questions but they are fundamental to the success of policy and practice in the early years. For the sake of this debate we will assume that a desired result of the earliest stage in a child's education and care is an independent, strong, competent, reflective and engaged child; one who is respected and cherished. David Whitebread's research findings highlighted several key elements that would be needed to enable such a purpose to be realised. These were:

- child-initiated activities
- unsupervised learning
- collaborative activities and talk.

All of which are in notably short supply during formal schooling. These findings lead back to aspects of developmentally friendly practices that have been discussed in earlier chapters. Children who are likely to become autonomous and self-regulated learners will be learning in ways that are active, interactive and independent. Chapters 2, 3 and 4 have explored both the theory and practice involved in learning collaboratively, unsupervised and actively. These ways of learning, if followed and built on in mainstream schooling, will support children's natural development and enable the characteristics we have been examining to flourish further.

Children do not flourish when coping with inconsistency, and the huge pedagogical gap between the Foundation Stage and key stage one is often a hard one for children to accommodate. Suddenly they are not asked to question, to explore or to work independently but find themselves in a culture where they need to find right answers. They are spending long periods of time sitting still and engaged in activities that have little meaning for them. Cognitive development does not thrive in such a context. This pedagogy is based on the theory of preparing children for the skills they will need as adults rather than giving them the tools they need now as young children.

The current philosophy of schools, which is based on preparation and thus concentrates on treating children as adults of tomorrow rather than as people of today, does significant damage to their cognitive processes. Children will become only too aware of the skills they are expected to have but which they have not yet acquired, in particular those associated with literacy and numeracy. Once the awareness has been confirmed by daily failure, many children become disaffected from schooling and make the not unreasonable assumption that learning is not for them. These are the same children who will fail to thrive in an inappropriately formal academic environment and may well go on to truant.

To foster a consistency in the learning environment, schools need to consider the following:

- There should be a seamless transition between nursery and reception; they work to the same curriculum.
- Children who do not fit the fixed standard should not be seen as 'behind'.

- Schools should consider whether they are ready for children and not the other way round.
- Most European children start formal schooling at six while UK English children enter reception at age four.
- If a child is found to be faring poorly in formal school the solution needs to be found in what the school is offering.
- For young children, the context, the environment in which learning happens, is all-important.

Perhaps the last word on this area of discussion should go to the writer of a letter, published in a national newspaper a few months ago. It said:

> Something else to thank Stephen Hawking for: his revelation that he didn't learn to read until he was eight. Like the vast majority of his contemporaries in the rest of Europe, he learned when he was ready, not at the force-fed rate that is still the norm in our own misguided education system.[14]

Challenges and dilemmas

- Clarify practitioners' thinking about what the needs of their children really are and separate them from what the setting's needs are. Write each set of needs on a separate list and ensure that the needs of the children are prioritised.
- Support families who are anxious about getting their children ready for school. Help them to resist the mass publications of formulaic work books that are being marketed to parents as a necessary part of the preparation process.

Epilogue

The aim of this book has been to help practitioners link the theory of children's cognitive development to the practice they see every day in their settings. This strand has been separated out from all other related strands of development only for ease of study and it is hoped that the examples of practice demonstrate how interlinked and indivisible all the developmental areas are in reality.

In examining one aspect of development in detail it has been possible to concentrate on ways in which young children learn, rather than the content of the curriculum. The emphasis has been on the characteristics of effective learning both of children themselves and of their learning environment. Together, these support their struggle to make sense of their world and engage them deeply in the treasure hunt that is inciting new understanding. It is a book that has aimed to look out at the world from inside a child's head rather than from the outside looking in. This ability to see the world from the child's point of view is possibly the early year's specialist's most valuable asset as it enables him or her to structure the learning context in ways that complement children's natural development rather than hindering it.

It is hoped that this text will give practitioners the knowledge and the courage they need to teach in ways that makes sense to children. If they do, their labours will be most effective, both in producing knowledgeable and skilful children and also in producing people with a life-long positive disposition to keep on learning.

Notes

Introduction to the series

1 National Association for the Education of Young Children. Position statement. 2009.
2 DfES. *The Early Years Foundation Stage*. London: DfES, 2007.

Introduction to *The Thinking Child*

1 M. Evangelou, K. Sylva and M. Kyriacou. *Early Years Learning and Development Literature Review*. London: Department for Children, Schools and Families, 2009. (Endnotes)

1 Setting the scene

1 Hugh Cunningham, *The Invention of Childhood*. BBC Books, 2006.
2 Hugh Cunningham, *The Invention of Childhood*. BBC Books, 2006.
3 David Wood,, *How Children Think and Learn*, second edition. Oxford: Blackwell, 1998.
4 Iram Siraj-Blatchford et al., *Researching Effective Pedagogy in the Early Years*. DfES, 2002.
5 Rosemary Roberts, *Self-esteem and Early Learning*, 2nd edition. Paul Chapman, 2002.
6 Helen Oxenbury, *The Three Little Wolves and the Big Bad Pig*. Egmont, 1993.
7 G. Dahlberg, P. Moss and A. R. Pence, *Beyond Quality in Early Years Education and Care*. Routledge/Falmer, 1999.
8 Angela Anning, *The First Years at School*, second edition. Buckingham: Open University Press, 1999.
9 *The Early Years: Foundations for Life, Health and Learning*. Report on the Early Years Foundation Stage by Dame Clare Tickell to Her Majesty's Government, 2011.

2 Playing, exploring and learning

1 Report on the Early Years Foundation Stage by Dame Clare Tickell to Her Majesty's Government, 2011.
2 J. Fisher, *Starting from the Child?* Buckingham: Open University Press, 1996.
3 Kathy Sylva, Carolyn Roy and Grant McIntyre, *Child Watching at Playgroup and Nursery School*. London: Grant McIntyre, 1980.
4 Department of Children, Schools and Families, Qualifications and Development Agency, *Learning, Playing and Interacting: Good Practice in the Early Years Foundation Stage*, 2009. Ref 00775-2009BKT-EN.
5 Alan Bainbridge, *Children's Learning in the New Early Years Professional*, (ed.) Angela D. Nurse. Abingdon: Routledge, 2007.
6 M. K. Smith, 'Jerome Bruner and the Process of Education', *Encyclopaedia of Informal Education*, 2002. http://www.infed.org/thinkers/bruner.htm

7   EYFS card 4.3.
8   Loris Malaguzzi, 'The Hundred Languages of Children', in C. Edwards, L. Gansini and G. Foreman (eds), *The Hundred Languages of Children: The Reggio Emilia Approach.* Greenwich, CT and London: Ablex, 1998.

3 Active learning

1   Dorothy Cohen, *The Learning Child.* Random House, 1972.
2   Ferre Leavers, *The Project Experiential Education.* Leuven: Katholieke Universiteit, 1999.
3   M. Carr, 'Being a Learner: Five Learning Dispositions for Early Childhood', *Early Childhood Practice* 1.1 (1999), pp. 81–99.
4   C. Nutbrown, *Threads of Thinking Young Children Learning and the Role of Education.* London: Sage, 2006.

4 Creating and thinking critically

1   In C. Griffin Beale (ed.), *Christian Schiller in His Own Words.* A. & C Black, 1979.
2   J. Dunn, 'Children's Relationships: Bridging the Divide between Cognitive and Social Development'. The Emmanuel Miller memorial lecture 1995. *Journal of Child Psychology and Psychiatry* 37.
3   D. Wood, *How Children Think and Learn.* Oxford: Blackwell, 1998.
4   L. J. Schweinhart, 'The High/Scope Preschool Curriculum Comparison Study through Age 23', *Early Childhood Research Quarterly* 12.
5   Helen Oxenbury, *The Three Little Wolves and the Big Bad Pig.* Egmont, 1993.
6   DFES, 2007, EYFS card 4.3.
7   K. Sylva, E. Melhuish, P. Sammons, I. Siraj-Blatchford and B. Taggart, *The Effective Provision of Pre-School Education.* DfES, 2004.
8   Rosie Roberts, *Self-esteem and Early Learning.* London: Hodder and Stoughton, 1995.

5 Observing and assessing children's progress

1   'Observing Children', in S. Smidt (ed.), *The Early Years: A Reader.* London: Routledge, 1998.
2   D. Rich, D. Casanova, A. Dixon, M. J. Drummond, A. Durrant and C. Myer, *First Hand Experience: What Matters to Children.* Rich Learning Opportunities, 2008.
3   Jacqui Cousins, *Listening to Four Year Olds.* London: Early Years Network, 2003.
4   K. Sylva, *Journal of Child Psychology and Psychiatry* 35.1 (1994), pp. 135–70.
5   Bernadette Duffy, *Supporting Creativity and Imagination in the Early Years.* Buckingham: Open University Press, 1998.
6   M. Evangelou, K. Sylva, A. Edwards and T. Smith, *Supporting Parents in Promoting Early Learning: The Evaluation of the Early Learning Partnership Project.* DCSF Research Report RR039. Nottingham: Department for Children, Schools and Families, 2008.
7   *The Early Years: Foundations for Life, Health and Learning.* Report on the Early Years Foundation Stage by Dame Clare Tickell to Her Majesty's Government, 2011.
8   M. J. Drummond, *Assessing Children's Learning.* London: David Fulton, 1993.
9   EYFS Statutory Framework, p. 16.
10 Jennie Lindon, 'Analysis: EYFS Assessment isn't about Paperwork', *Nursery World*, 2008.
11 C. Pascal and P. Bertram, 'Assessing what Matters in the Early Years', in J. Fisher (ed.), *Foundations of Learning.* Buckingham: Open University Press, 2002.
12 Christopher Ball, *The Importance of Early Learning: Start Right Report.* London: Royal Society for Arts, 1994.

6 Partnerships with parents and community

1 Margaret Carr, 'What is Effective Assessment? A View from New Zealand', paper presented on effective assessment and evaluation in the early years, Penn Green.
2 M. Evangelou, S. Sylva, M. Kyriacou, M. Wild and G. Glenny, Research report DCSF-RR176.
3 A. N. Schore, 'Foreword', in J. Bowlby, *Attachment and Loss*, Vol. 1. New York: Basic Books, 1999.
4 M. Robinson, *Development 0-8: A Journey Through the Early Years*. Maidenhead: Open University Press, 2008.
5 B. Tizzard and M. Hughes, *Young Children Learning: Thinking and Talking in the Home*. London: Fontana, 1984.
6 Margaret Donaldson, *Children's Minds*. London: Fontana, 1978.
7 P. Munn and H. R. Schaffer, 'Literacy and Numeracy Events in Social Interactive Contexts', *International Journal of Early Years Education* 1.3.
8 *Sunday Times*, 6 May 2012.
9 E. C. Melhuish, B. Mai, M. P. Phan, K. Sylva, P. Sammons, I. Siraj-Blatchford and B. Taggart, 'Effects of Home Learning Environment and Preschool Centre Experience upon Literacy and Numeracy Development in Early Primary School', *Journal of Social Issues* 64.1 (2008).
10 H. Wheeler, J. Conner and H. Goodwin, *Parents, Early Years and Learning: Parents as Partners in the Early Years Foundation Stage: Principles into Practice*. London: National Children's Bureau, 2009.
11 P. May, E. Ashford and G. Bottle, *Sound Beginnings*. London: David Fulton, 2006.

7 Thinking differently

1 EYFS card 1.2.
2 G. Dahlberg, P. Moss and A. Pence, *Beyond Quality in Early Childhood Education and Care: Postmodern Perspectives*. London: Routledge/Falmer, 1999.
3 L. Katz, *Dispositions as Educational Goals*. ERIC Digest ED36345 1993-09-00.
4 C. S. Dweck and E. L. Leggett, 'A Social-Cognitive Approach to Motivation and Personality', *Psychological Review* 95 (1988), pp. 256–73.
5 J. Linden, *Understanding Child Development: Linking Theory and Practice*. Abingdon: Hodder Arnold, 2005, p. 105.
6 Margaret Mayo, illustrated by Alan Ayliffe, *Dig, Dig, Digger*. New York: Henry Holt and Co.
7 *In G. W. Evans and M. A. Schamberg, 'Childhood Poverty, Chronic Stress, and Adult Working Memory', Proceedings of the National Academy of Sciences 106.13 (30 March 2009).*

8 Thoughtful organisation

1 M. Edgington, *The Foundation Stage Teacher in Action*, 3rd edition. Paul Chapman Publishing, 2004.
2 DES, *Starting With Quality* (The Rumbold Report). London: Department of Education and Science, 1990.
3 Julie Fisher, *Starting from the Child*. Buckingham: Open University Press, 1996.
4 Janet Moyles and Maulfrey Worthington, 'The Early Years Foundation Stage through the Daily Experiences of Children'. TACTYC Occasional Paper no.1, 2011. http://www.tactyc.org.uk
5 P. May, 'Water Play'. Unpublished MA, Oxford Brookes University, 2000.
6 I. Siraj-Blatchford *et al.*, 2002, *Researching Effective Pedagogy in the Early Years* (REPEY). DfES.

9 Equipped for life, ready for school?

1 *Children and their Primary Schools* (The Plowden Report). HMSO, 1967, p. 187.
2 Julie Fisher, *Moving on to Key Stage One*. Buckingham: Open University Press, 2010.
3 G. Claxton, *Can Schools Prepare you for Anything?* Graham Nuthall Annual Lecture, University of Canterbury NZ, 2012.

4 Janet Moyles and Maulfry Worthington, "The Early Years Foundation Stage through the Daily Experiences of Children." TACTYC, 2011.

5 EYFS card 4.1.

6 S. Adams, E. Alexander, M. J. Drummond and J. Moyles, 'Inside the Foundation Stage: Recreating the Reception Year'. Final Report. London: ATL.

7 *The Early Years: Foundations for Life, Health and Learning*, pp. 87–88.

8 DfES, 2007.

9 Tickell Report, p. 20.

10 S. Adams, E. Alexander and M. Drummond, *Inside the Foundation Stage*. Association of Teachers and Lecturers, 2004.

11 Association for the Professional Development of Early Years Practitioners, David Whitebread and Sue Bingham, University of Cambridge, 2011.

12 *Starting with Quality*. Department of Education and Science. London: HMSO.

13 TACTYC Occasional Paper no. 2: 'School Readiness: A Critical Review of Perspectives and Evidence'.

14 *The Guardian*, 11 January 2012.

Author index

Subject index